Garnered and Garnished by

DOUGLAS G. MELDRUM

CHARLES SCRIBNER'S SONS

New York   London   Toronto   Sydney   Tokyo   Singapore

The Night 2,000 Men Came to Dinner

and Other Appetizing Anecdotes

CHARLES SCRIBNER'S SONS
Rockefeller Center
1230 Avenue of the Americas
New York, NY 10020

Designed by Chris Welch

Manufactured in the United States of America

1 3 5 7 9 10 8 6 4 2

Library of Congress Cataloging-in-Publication Data
Meldrum, Douglas G.
The night 2,000 men came to dinner and other appetizing anecdotes /
garnered and garnished by Douglas G. Meldrum.
p.   cm.
1. Food—Anecdotes.   2. Gastronomy—Anecdotes.   3. Celebrities—
Anecdotes.   I. Title.   II. Title: Night two thousand men came to dinner and
other appetizing anecdotes.
TX357.M45   1994   94-14035
641'.01'3—dc20   CIP
ISBN 0-02-583960-8

With love to B.T.M., who
gives so much and
asks for so little

Contents

The Banquet, *from* The Election Series, *by William Hogarth (1697–1764)*.

Food and Eating, Drink and Drinking in the Lives of Some of the Great Movers and Shakers of All Time

The achievement of fame and fortune, success and power, does not always lead to refinement in eating and drinking.

At the outset—to lay a foundation, so to speak—it is appropriate that guidance on table manners be heard from a scholar whose reputation for greatness has withstood the test of time.

In 1530, DESIDERIUS ERASMUS, which means "Desired Beloved," wrote a book, *On Civility in Children*, for the ten-year-old French prince who became King Henry II. The book was widely successful, was translated into English in 1532, and included some basic directions on proper behavior at the dining table:

♀ Take care to cut and clean your fingernails before dining; otherwise dirt from under the nails may get into the food.

♀ Don't be the first to reach into the pot; only wolves and gluttons do that.

♀ Take the first piece of meat or fish that you touch, and don't poke around in the pot for a bigger one.

♀ Don't pick your nose while eating and then reach for more food.

♀ Don't clean your teeth with your knife.

♀ If your fingers become greasy, it is not polite to lick them or wipe them on your coat. Bring a cloth along for this purpose if your host does not provide one. Or else wipe them on the tablecloth.

3

Three hundred years after Erasmus, but well before **EMILY POST** or **MISS MANNERS**, a nineteenth-century artist presented eleven examples of bad manners in a single illustration:

BAD MANNERS AT TABLE

1. Tips back his chair.

2. Eats with his mouth too full.

3. Feeds a dog at the table.

4. Holds his knife improperly.

5. Engages in violent argument at mealtime.

6. Lounges upon the table.

7. Brings a cross child to the table.

8. Drinks from the saucer, and laps with his tongue the last drop from his plate.

9. Comes to the table in his shirtsleeves, and puts his feet beside his chair.

10. Picks his teeth with his fingers.

11. Scratches her head and is frequently unnecessarily getting up from the table.

5

ISAAC NEWTON (1642–1727) probably had perfectly good table manners, but sometimes he became so preoccupied with deep thoughts that he forgot whether or not he had eaten, a mental lapse some dinner guests considered rude. Such an incident was described by Louis Figuier:

> Newton's friend Dr. Stukely came to dinner with him. After waiting a long time for him to come out of his study, the doctor decided to help himself to some of the chicken that was already on the table. When he had finished, he left the remains of the bird on the plate and covered it with the silver cover. At the end of several hours, Newton finally made his appearance, saying that he was very hungry. He sat down at the table and lifted the cover from the chicken, but when he saw the carcass, "I thought," he cried, "I had not yet dined. I see I was mistaken."

THE EARL OF SANDWICH, an enthusiastic cardplayer, found that he could eat meat between two pieces of bread without interrupting his play. Having thus invented the sandwich, the earl, always a well-mannered gentleman, advised fellow cardplayers in 1722 that a sandwich should be eaten with "a civilized swallow and not a barbarous bolt."

Socialite WILLIAM VINCENT ASTOR, who died in 1959, had a strange sense of humor. He thought it highly amusing and entertaining to hire an actor to pose as a waiter, spill soup on a chosen dinner guest, and then insult him.

ALFRIED KRUPP (1907–1967), last of a long line of sole owners of the German industrial dynasty that began in 1587, had to tolerate his own special privations during World War II in the Krupp castle that overlooked the immense Krupp munitions plant, where slave laborers toiled and starved, fighting over rats and mice they caught for food. In *The Arms of Krupp*, William Manchester describes events during a Royal Air Force bombing raid:

The soup was late. He (Alfried) looked annoyed. Then the maître *did the unforgivable; he served a Moselle with meat. Alfried eyed his pale glass and inquired what had become of the red wines. The* maître *explained; there had been a brief fire in the servants' quarters. Krupp's eyebrows shot up: what did the fire have to do with* der Wein? *Fidgeting, the* maître *stammered out that a bomb had hit a pipe. The castle had no water. The castle owner's forehead remained crinkled. How, he asked, had the blaze been brought under control?* "Mit dem Châteauneuf-du-Pape," *the wretched man mumbled. Alfried stared at him incredulously, and, like a member of the Reform Club, murmured,* "Nicht möglich! Extraordinär. Das ist aber wirklich zu viel." *("Indeed! Extraordinary. Really, this is too much.") He toyed with a solid gold fork, toyed with a solid gold spoon—then solemnly tasted the white wine.* "Ach so, er ist gut," *he said quietly. Dinner proceeded without further incident.*

BRILLAT-SAVARIN, also known as Jean Anthelme, was a lawyer and a politician. He published various pamphlets on the law, but it was *La Physiologie du goût,* published shortly before his death in 1826, that brought him fame. Considered one of the best and most influential gastronomical works in existence, *La Physiologie du goût* sets down these rules to ensure a perfect meal:

♈ That the number of guests does not exceed a dozen, so that conversation can constantly be general.

♈ That they should be carefully chosen, that their professions be different but their tastes similar and with such points of contact that one will not have to resort to the odious formality of presentations.

♈ That the dining room be luxuriously lit, the cloth be of the utmost cleanliness, and the temperature from thirteen to sixteen degrees by the Réaumur thermometer [sixty-one to sixty-six degrees F.].

♈ That the men be witty without pretensions and the women charming without being too coquettish.

♈ That the choice of dishes should be exquisite but restrained in number and the wines be of the first quality, each the best of its kind.

♈ That the order, for the former, should be from the most substantial to the lightest and, for the latter, from the lightest to those with the greatest bouquet.

♈ That the speed of eating should be moderate, dinner being the last affair of the day, and that the guests behave like travelers who aim to arrive at the same destination together.

BRILLAT-SAVARIN had additional rules of etiquette in a more philosophical vein:

- Those who give themselves indigestion or get drunk do not know how to eat or drink.
- The most indispensable quality of a cook is punctuality; it should also be that of a guest.
- To wait too long for a latecomer is to show a lack of consideration for all those present.
- He who receives his friends and gives no personal attention to the meal that is being prepared for them is not worthy of having friends.
- To invite someone is to take charge of his happiness during the time he spends under your roof.

Brillat-Savarin (1755–1826), French politician and gastronomist.

DANIEL WEBSTER (1782–1852), American lawyer, orator, statesman, literary giant, congressman, senator, Secretary of State, and perennial presidential candidate, was born in 1782 and had a privileged upbringing. His father was a tavernkeeper at a time when such places in New England were closely regulated and only respected community leaders, usually retired military officers, were licensed to own them.

Webster went to Phillips Exeter Academy and Dartmouth College, where he gained early recognition as an orator and an appreciation for fine wine. When he was in his fifties and a prominent public figure, his drinking, sometimes justifiably, was used against him politically. At times his behavior, at the very least, was questionable. According to Irvin H. Bartlett in the biography *Daniel Webster:*

> *A senator's daughter remembered going to tea with the Websters and then on to the opera. Webster had drunk a lot but seemed normal enough until in the midst of the performance he suddenly leaped to his feet and belted out a few bars of "Hail Columbia, Happy Land" before his wife could grab his coattails and pull him back down again. The anecdote of Webster at one of Jenny Lind's concerts, and how he insisted on standing up in the front row and taking every bow with her, was another favorite around Washington. At Webster's death, the rumors about his drinking had become so numerous that his physician and many friends and acquaintances felt called upon to testify that they had never seen him drunk. What most of these statements really say is that Webster could hold his liquor. We must remember, of course, that Webster grew up at a time when wine and whiskey were almost universally approved*

and even taken liberally by ministers. Other politicians of his generation, like Silas Wright and Henry Clay, were famous drinkers, and at a cold-water banquet in Boston after Webster's second Bunker Hill address, President John Tyler frequently ducked under the table to consult a flask of brandy.

Daniel Webster's drinking was used effectively by political cartoonists to ridicule him in his later years. (From The Lantern, *New York, 1852)*

Little is known of the food preferences of **JOAN OF ARC** (1412–1431), but a close friend described her as she prepared for battle:

She only had wine poured in a silver cup, in which she put half water and five or six "soupes" *which she ate and did not take anything else.*

The *"soupes"* were slices of bread which, in the Middle Ages, were eaten with meat and vegetables by dipping them into the juices.

CAPTAIN JOHN SMITH, pioneering colonist, described tamale pie as it was made by the Indians in Virginia in 1612:

Their corne they rost in the eare greene, and bruising it in a mortar of wood with a Polt, lappe it in the rowled leaves of their corne, and so boyle it for a daintie.

ANN LEE (1736–1784) founded the Shakers; it is traditional for them to commemorate her birthday by holding an afternoon meeting followed by supper at which Mother Ann's Birthday Cake is served. The original recipe advises:

Cut a handful of peach twigs which are filled with sap at this season of the year (February). Clip the ends and bruise them and beat the cake batter with them. This will impart a delicate peach flavor to the cake.

. . . and here, which I never did before, I drank a glass, of a pint. I believe, at one draught, of the juice of Oranges of whose peel they make comfits; and here they drink the juice as wine, with sugar, and it is a very fine drink; but it being new, I was doubtful whether it might not do me hurt.

Diary of Samuel Pepys
March 9, 1669

Note: Orange and lemon juice were rarely drunk. Lemonade is said to have been mentioned first in Thomas Killegrew's Parson's Wedding, published in 1663.

ANTOINE-AUGUSTIN PARMENTIER, an eighteenth-century French agriculturalist, was convinced that the potato, though looked upon with suspicion, could play a major role in solving his country's food problems. Parmentier knew the value of good public relations and, before the French Revolution, sent Louis XVI a bouquet of potato flowers for his birthday. The flowers caught the eye of the queen, Marie Antoinette, and she put some in her hair. Immediately it became fashionable to wear potato blossoms in the lapel or hair, and the potato was on its way to becoming a staple in France.

Potato plant.
(John Parkinson,
Paradisi in Sole, *1629)*

Parmentier showing his first crop of potatoes to Louis XVI. (North Wind Picture Archives)

In 1777, an Englishman named GREY opened a condiment shop in Dijon, France, and began selling mustard. Later, POUPON, a Frenchman, joined the business and "Moutarde Grey-Poupon" became famous. Heublein, Inc., introduced the product to the United States in 1946; today, distributed under Nabisco Brands, it is the nation's biggest seller of all premium-priced mustards.

(Courtesy Nabisco Inc.)

Novelist **WILLIAM DEAN HOWELLS** (1837–1920) recalled in 1894 a breakfast in Boston with James T. Fields, Oliver Wendell Holmes's publisher, saying:

> *I remember his burlesque pretence that morning of an inextinguishable grief when I owned that I had never eaten blueberry cake before, and how he kept returning to the pathos of the fact that there should be a region of the earth [Howells was born in Ohio] where blueberry cake was unknown.*

JOHN D. ROCKEFELLER who was born in 1839, had a classic dish named for his wealth rather than for himself. The story is that at Antoine's, the famous New Orleans restaurant, a customer was served some oysters prepared in a special way, prompting him to exclaim with delight, "Why, this is as rich as Rockefeller!" Thus, "Oysters Rockefeller."

Inventor THOMAS ALVA EDISON (1847–1931) ate irregularly and followed fad diets. At one time he existed on sardines, prunes, and dry toast.

There are several stories about why doughnuts have holes in the center, including the unlikely claim by the Wampanoag Indian tribe that an arrow aimed at a Pilgrim housewife missed her and pierced a fried cake she was making. Another story, accepted as gospel by the hardy seafaring men of Maine, is that CAPTAIN HANSON CROCKETT GREGORY in 1847 was fighting a violent storm while trying to bring his ship, the *Frypan,* to port. With a doughnut in one hand, Gregory struggled with the ship's wheel with the other. An especially huge wave washed over the deck, and the captain, reluctant to lose his doughnut to grip the wheel with both hands, rammed it down over a spoke in the wheel, pushing out the center. When things calmed down a little, the good captain retrieved his doughnut from the wheel spoke and finished eating it. Word spread rapidly of Gregory's coolness and ingenuity and it became traditional for doughnuts aboard vessels sailing from harbors in Maine to have holes in the center.

GAIL BORDEN was inspired to work on milk preservation on a transatlantic voyage. The son of a frontiersman, Borden went to London in 1852 to the International Exposition to sell a dehydrated meat biscuit he had invented. He used all the money he could beg or borrow to put his invention across and was forced to travel in steerage class when he returned to America. On the ship he was appalled by the conditions he saw. Entire families of immigrants from eastern and southern Europe were crowded in miserable quarters and en route several infants died in their mothers' arms, sickened by the milk of infected cows carried aboard to furnish milk, butter, and cream for the passengers. Some way, Borden felt, should be developed to preserve milk for long voyages.

Many before him had worked on the problem of milk preservation, including Louis Pasteur. It took Borden four years to perfect his process for condensing milk and then to prove its worth to skeptics. Finally, in 1856, his patent was approved and the first canned milk was introduced on the American market.

Borden's condensed milk is still a best-seller, 138 years after its introduction.

SYLVESTER GRAHAM, an American reformer, lectured extensively in the early 1800s, urging, among other things, the use of unsifted whole wheat flour. Graham flour is still on the market today and graham crackers are still an American favorite. Graham had other convictions, including the belief that fats led to sexual excesses and that condiments such as mustard, ketchup, and pepper led to insanity. He practiced what he preached and did not eat red meat, fatty foods, or white bread. He did not drink alcohol, exercised regularly, and bathed and brushed his teeth frequently, but died when he was fifty-seven.

*Sylvester Graham's name lives on—
on packages of popular products.
(Photo by Meldrum)*

(Courtesy Nabisco Inc.)

In 1863, two Fort Wayne, Indiana, druggists, THOMAS BIDDLE and JAMES HOAGLAND, mixed baking soda with cream of tartar to produce a new product, which eventually was marketed internationally as ROYAL Baking Powder.

Inventive minds have worked on the problems of food preservation and distribution throughout history and, as is usually the case, the solution to one problem led to the creation of another.

In 1810, Parisian NICHOLAS APPERT, in *L'Art de Conserver*, described how fruit, vegetables, and meat could be put in bottles, then raised to a temperature high enough to destroy bacteria. The problem of bottle breakage was overcome by the Englishman PETER DURAND, who developed canisters of tin-lined iron that preserved food but were very heavy and almost impossible to open. Lighter cans of steel were introduced in the 1850s along with various devices to open them, none of which worked very well. In 1858, EZRA WARNER was granted a patent for an implement that set the pace for can openers until a cutting "wheel" was introduced. It wasn't until the 1960s that self-opening cans were introduced, first with tabs that separated from the cans and were thrown away, creating an environmental hazard. Credit is given to ERMAN FRAZER for the design of a can with an "inseparable tear strip" that allowed the user to drink directly from the can without cutting his lips or hitting his nose on the tab.

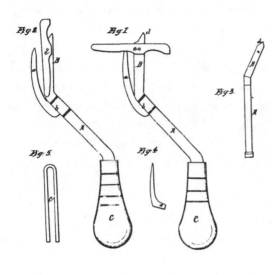

Can opener patented in 1858 by Ezra Warner minimized many of the previous difficulties— and dangers—of "getting at" the contents of the tough tins. (U.S. Patent Office)

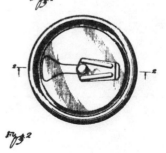

Erman Frazer patented this design in 1963 for a self-opening can. (U.S. Patent Office)

WILLIAM PAINTER probably had no idea of the problems he created with his invention of a bottle cap manufactured under U.S. Patent Number 468,226, granted on February 2, 1892. The cap consisted of a piece of tin with a cork insert and a corrugated rim or skirt that was crimped around the neck of the bottle. This provided a superb seal but one that was virtually impossible to get off without a special opener. Openers were attached to coolers and dispensing machines, in hotel and motel rooms, and given away by manufacturers, all adding to the cost of the beverage. The screw top was finally developed, but became associated with less expensive beers; many premium beers still retain the old cap requiring an opener.

There are literally hundreds of devices on the market today for getting corks out of bottles. One of the most reliable still in wide use was designed by M. L. BYRN of New York City, who was awarded U.S. Patent Number 27,615 on March 27, 1860, for a gimlet screw with a T handle—a corkscrew.

MOSES COATES, a mechanic from Downington, Pennsylvania, was granted a patent for an apple corer on February 14, 1803.

An early apple corer/peeler.
(From a nineteenth-century catalog)

In 1865, a young Austrian, **CHARLES FLEISCHMANN**, came to America to attend his sister's wedding and was astonished by the poor flavor of American bread. Back in Austria, he collected samples of yeast used to bake Viennese bread and, returning to America, formed a company to produce this country's first standardized yeast, a product that revolutionized baking in America.

WILLIAM FINLEY SEMPLE of Mount Vernon, Ohio, was awarded U.S. Patent Number 98,304 on December 28, 1869, for a "combination of rubber with other articles, in any proportion adapted to the formation of an acceptable chewing gum."

More than twenty years earlier, in 1848, JOHN CURTIS and his brother in Bangor, Maine, were manufacturing "State of Maine Pure Spruce Gum" on a Franklin stove. In 1850 they moved to Portland, Maine, and made paraffin gums under the brand names "Licorice Lulu," "Four-in-Hand," "Sugar Cream," "Biggest and Best," and "White Mountain." They also produced spruce gums named "Yankee Spruce," "American Flag," "Trunk Spruce," and "200 Lump Spruce."

ALEXANDER CAMPBELL, a Brooklyn, New York, milkman, delivered milk in glass bottles for the first time on January 11, 1878. Previously milk was sold "loose": customers brought containers to the milkman, who ladled out the quantity wanted.

In the 1930s a battle began between glass and wax-coated paper milk containers and, in 1948, a plastic-coated carton was introduced. By 1961, wax- and plastic-coated cartons accounted for over 60 percent of all milk containers, with the last bastion of the glass bottle being for home delivery. Today, the glass milk bottle is as extinct as the horse-drawn cart with a large milk canister and dipper on the back.

New in 1878, newer in 1930.
(Archive Photos/Welgos)

(Courtesy Nabisco Inc.)

BARNUM'S ANIMAL CRACKERS were produced in England for many years before they were introduced in America in 1902. They became a part of the national scene and prompted the *New York Evening Journal* to say that "zoos in some of our cities are so incomplete that the only way a lot of kids can learn anything about wild beasts is from Animal Crackers."

Trivia buffs should note that a box of Animal Crackers contains seventeen separate animals: bear (sitting and walking), bison, camel, cougar, elephant, giraffe, hippopotamus, hyena, kangaroo, lion, monkey, rhinoceros, seal, sheep, tiger, and zebra.

In 1902, CLARENCE CRANE, a Cleveland, Ohio, chocolate manufacturer, decided to do something to maintain the volume of his business when the demand for chocolate fell off during the hot months. He began producing a hard candy that stayed fresh and appetizing no matter how high the temperature. He hired a pill maker to press his mints into a circle with a hole in the middle and named them LIFE SAVERS. Crane was selling his new product locally as a summer substitute for his chocolates when New York advertising man EDWARD NOBLE bought the rights to the new candy for $2,900.

(Courtesy Nabisco Inc.)

In 1914, CLARENCE BIRDSEYE was a twenty-eight-year-old scientist on an expedition for the U.S. Fish and Wildlife Service in Labrador. An avid fisherman, "Bob" Birdseye was amazed to discover that as soon as he pulled a fish from a hole in the Arctic ice and exposed it to the air, it froze instantly. He also found that the fish could be kept in their frozen state for weeks, then defrosted and cooked without losing their flavor.

Emulating the Eskimos, Birdseye buried caribou steaks in ice and found they tasted great when he broiled them much later. He experimented with vegetables, plunging cabbages into a barrel of ice-cold water where they froze immediately. When he cooked them later in boiling water, he was excited to discover that they retained their fresh flavor.

World War I interrupted his experiments, but after the war he went into the fishing business in Gloucester, Massachusetts, and, on the side, continued to freeze fish. He was convinced that the key was to freeze them quickly at temperatures well below zero.

Birdseye used his quick-freezing methods for many foodstuffs—raw meats, vegetables, fruits, fish, even cooked foods such as cakes, pies, and breads. To raise capital he served frozen dinners to potential investors. One tycoon was persuaded to invest when Birdseye sent a complete frozen dinner for four to his home in New York.

Once he had financial backing, Birdseye started to merchandise his "quick-frozen" foods on a national scale. Freezer cabinets were offered free to stores willing to stock the foods, which were displayed in colorful packages with clear instructions for their preparation. A national newspaper campaign was launched, and the first Birdseye foods went on sale in 1930. The nation was in a period of economic depression and Birdseye's products were much more expensive than fresh foods; furthermore, they had to be prepared in a way that was new to American housewives. Yet within ten years they were in such demand that virtually all segments of the giant food industry followed Birdseye's lead. Other companies began to enter the frozen food business to satisfy the demand for out-of-season foods that tasted "fresh," not canned.

C. R. TAYLOR was granted a patent for an ice-cream-cone rolling machine on January 29, 1924.

HENRY W. JEFFERS invented a rotating milking platform that was installed in the lactorium of the Walker Gordon Laboratory Company, Inc., at Plainsboro, New Jersey, on November 13, 1930. The new concept permitted 1,680 cows to be milked in seven hours by means of a revolving platform that brought the cows into position with the milking machines. It was known as the "Rotolactor."

"That's the best thing since sliced bread" was a very popular expression during World War II, but it is a little difficult to pin down exactly who should be thanked for inventing a machine to slice large numbers of loaves of bread. In 1871 a patent was granted to JOHN CURRIER of Springfield, Massachusetts, for a bread slicer, but it wasn't until 1930 that precut bread hit the mass market when Continental Baking adopted a machine developed by OTTO FREDERICK ROHWEDDER for "Wonder Bread," a household word during the Depression. By 1933, 80 percent of the bread sold in the United States was presliced.

Rohwedder had been working on his bread slicer since 1912. After various versions, including one that held the slices together with sterile hairpins to preserve freshness and another that packed the slices in shallow boxes, in 1928 he came up with a machine that simply sliced the loaf on its way to the automatic wrapper.

The *Wall Street Journal* paid tribute to Rohwedder when he died, saying at the conclusion of the article: "Rohwedder, who never became affluent or famous, died in a Michigan rest home on November 8, 1960, at the age of eighty. Modern versions of his slicer live on."

BEER IN CANS was sold for the first time on January 24, 1935, in Richmond, Virginia.

JOHN BROWN, the fanatical abolitionist, staged his historic raid on Harpers Ferry, Virginia, on October 16, 1859, and seized the Wagner House Hotel, the federal arsenal, the town firehouse, and some thirty townspeople. Brown's objective, he said, was to free the nation's slaves and establish them in an independent Negro republic. While the raid on Harpers Ferry was serious—and tragic—it was not without its lighter side. On the morning after the raid, Brown needed breakfast for his band of eighteen men and thirty prisoners. One of his prisoners was the bartender at the Wagner House, and the hotel's management offered to serve Brown forty-eight dishes of ham and eggs in exchange for their bartender. Brown accepted the offer.

GUSTAVUS D. DOWS installed a counter for serving beverages in his drugstore in Lowell, Massachusetts, on March 9, 1858. This was the grandfather of the soda fountain, which today is little more than a nostalgic memory.

Sentimental scene of Americans sipping sodas at the local drugstore, complete with soda "jerk." (Archive Photos/Camerique)

GENERAL THOMAS "STONEWALL" JACKSON (1824–1863) complained of "dyspepsia" all his life. He sucked lemons and ate standing up to relieve the condition. An eyewitness reported that during a raging battle Jackson went into the region of heavy fighting and

> *At that moment someone handed him a lemon . . . immediately a small piece was bitten out of it and slowly and unsparingly he began to extract its flavor and juice. From that moment until darkness, that lemon scarcely left his lips except to be used to emphasize an order. He listened to Yankee shout or Rebel yell, to the sounds of musketry . . . to all the signs of promise or apprehension, but he never for an instant lost his interest in that lemon. Once Jackson paused, his face calm as ever. "I think I never had a better lemon," he said.*

Understandably, the men in Jackson's regiment gave him the nickname "Lemon Squeezer."

For many years before he died at eighty-three in 1877, CORNELIUS VANDERBILT took time out from railroad tycooning to relax at Moon's Lake House in Saratoga Springs, New York. At lunch one day in 1853, Vanderbilt returned a serving of french-fried potatoes to George Crum, head chef at the resort, insisting that they be cut thinner and fried longer. Crum reacted angrily and cut some potatoes in paper-thin slices, soaked them in ice water, and fried them in deep fat. Much to Crum's surprise, Vanderbilt and his guests raved over the curled and crisp results and ordered more. From that day on "Saratoga Chips" were featured on the hotel's menu and potato chips were introduced to the world.

CORNELIUS VANDERBILT had a reputation for being stingy, which he maintained until the end. When he was on his deathbed, the attending physician prescribed a glass of Champagne for his patient. Frugal to the last, Cornelius waved the Champagne aside and croaked, "Won't sody-water do instead?"

CHARLES SCHWAB, steel magnate, dined regularly at the Ritz-Carlton in New York City and was the first person to be served a new soup developed by chef Louis Diat to celebrate the opening in 1910 of the roof garden at this prestigious hotel. Actually, Diat refined a traditional hot leek-and-potato peasant soup his mother used to make in France. Diat cooled the soup, added a liberal amount of cream, called it "Vichyssoise" after the fashionable water spa Vichy, and enjoyed the acclamation.

BUTCH CASSIDY was born Robert Leroy Parker in 1866. The notorious holdup man invented a drink before he killed himself. He called it the "Block and Tackle," explaining that if you take one drink and "walk a block, you will tackle anything." To make the drink, pour three ounces of whiskey into a glass; add one drop of anise and three drops of peppermint flavoring.

During World War I DOUGLAS MACARTHUR was in command of the 84th Brigade of the Rainbow Division in France when he made this entry in his diary:

Found a little patched-up inn in the village of Bulson, located at the foot of the heights, and asked for a meal. Proprietor had nothing but potatoes but what a feast he laid before me. Served them in five different courses—potato soup, potato fricassee, potatoes creamed, potato salad and I finished with potato pie. It may be because I have not eaten for thirty-six hours, but that meal seems about the best I have ever had. Gave the proprietor ten dollars and told him in my broken French he was a genius. He just about wept with delight.

In another war and on the other side of the world, Douglas MacArthur dines with his commander in chief, Franklin D. Roosevelt, in Hawaii in 1944. (AP/Wide World Photos)

The leading soft drink in the country in the 1920s was MOXIE, which, with sales of over 25 million cases a year, outsold Coca-Cola. Developed in 1876 by DR. AUGUSTIN THOMPSON in Lowell, Massachusetts, and called Moxie Nerve Food, it was a compound of gentian root extract, sassafras, and other herbs. It had a bitter, sour taste and, according to Dr. Thompson, would relieve "paralysis, softening of the brain, insanity, brain and nervous exhaustion, loss of manhood, imbecility, and helplessness."

Extensive point-of-purchase, billboard, and print advertising, featuring intense young men and pretty young women, kept Moxie on top of the beverage market for years. One of the most popular promotions around 1908 showed "The Feather Tickle Girl" (right).

In the 1920s Yale University students found a new way to amuse themselves between classes by throwing empty tin pie plates from a nearby bakery back and forth to each other. The name of the bakery, stamped on the round tins, was Frisbie, after WILLIAM RUSSELL FRISBIE, who opened the enterprise in the 1870s in Bridgeport, Connecticut. Some years after the game was invented at Yale, plastic disks were introduced bearing the trademark FRISBEE.

In 1931, JULIAN HUXLEY, the English biologist, went on a trip to the U.S.S.R. in an effort to bring British scientists and medical men in contact with their Russian colleagues. In his memoirs, Huxley said:

> We stayed [in Moscow] at the Hotel Europa, where we breakfasted early on a mug of tea without milk or sugar, a slab of horse-meat and a slice of rye bread. We sympathized with the growing pains of the regime, but were not very enthusiastic about our breakfasts.
>
> . . . Most days we sat down to our frugal "midday" meal at four in the afternoon. . . . Famished as well as exhausted, we ate all we were offered.
>
> Official banquets were another matter. In spite of the grievous food shortage, they were copious in the extreme—drinks and hors d'oeuvres comprising boar's head and suckling pig, tongue, salmon and sturgeon, caviar ad lib, and with roasts and sweets to follow. And, of course, much wine and vodka and many toasts, so that it was after midnight before we got back to our hotel. As we left, the women interpreters shovelled the remains of their dinner into large handbags—useful perks for their hungry families.

BOOKER T. WASHINGTON, the famous black educator, was invited by President Theodore Roosevelt to be a guest at dinner at the White House on October 18, 1901. This infuriated many sections of the South and caused several southern newspapers to attack both Roosevelt and Washington. The *Memphis Scimitar* (Tennessee) said that Roosevelt had "committed the most damnable outrage ever perpetrated by any citizen of the United States when he invited a nigger to dine with him at the White House."

JOSEPHUS DANIELS, Secretary of the Navy, stirred up a hornet's nest on June 1, 1914, when he issued an order forbidding the use of alcoholic beverages in the U.S. Navy.

BARRY M. GOLDWATER, (1909–) controversial senator and presidential candidate, was notorious for two habits: keeping the top of his desk immaculately clean and eating a cheeseburger supreme on that same desk for some fifteen years. "If I didn't have a luncheon engagement," Goldwater says in his autobiography, "the cheeseburger—topped with a slice of raw onion—would be waiting for me at my desk. I cleaned up the crumbs immediately. . . . I don't know if a spotless desk is the sign of a clean mind, but I was convinced that the smell of a cheeseburger supreme is not particularly conducive to airing official Senate business."

CAROLINE ASTOR was the unquestioned sovereign of New York society until her death in 1908 when she was seventy-seven years old. Doyenne of "the Four Hundred," she hosted the most extravagant and glamorous balls and dinners of the era.

On one occasion she covered her dinner table with several inches of sand in which she buried diamonds, sapphires, rubies, and emeralds. At each place setting there was a small sterling silver bucket with a spade to help guests "dig for treasure."

Gangster AL CAPONE was at his Palm Island estate in Miami, Florida, on St. Valentine's Day in 1929 entertaining more than a hundred sportswriters, gamblers, entertainers, racketeers, and politicians with an elaborate buffet and Champagne served by his bodyguards. As Capone played the gracious host in Florida his orders were being carried out in Chicago where, in the bloodiest massacre in gangland history, six racketeers and one bystander were riddled with bullets in a garage.

Capone enjoyed being in Florida and sometimes treated his cronies to picnics for which he would charter a seaplane for $160 an hour ($60 for the plane and $100 an hour for the pilot) to fly them to Bimini, where they would devour quantities of salami sandwiches and beer.

Capone had to be careful about what he ate because in 1923 the Aiellos, Capone's rivals in the bootlegging business, tried to have him poisoned. They offered the chef at Diamond Joe Esposito's Bella Napoli Café, one of Capone's favorite restaurants, $35,000 to flavor Capone's minestrone with prussic acid. At first the chef agreed, then had second thoughts and told Capone about the plot.

Chocolate chip cookies were created in 1933 because MRS. RUTH WAKEFIELD was running late and needed to speed up the process of making cookies for the guests at her Toll House Inn in Whitman, Massachusetts. To save time she decided that rather than melt chocolate before mixing it into her batter she would simply chop up the hard chocolate and let the bits melt as the cookies baked. The cookies were a sensation and, at first, Mrs. Wakefield called them chocolate crunch cookies. Later she changed the name to Toll House cookies.

RUDOLF HESS, who defected from Germany by flying to Scotland in 1941, was serving his sentence as a war criminal in Spandau Prison in 1963 when fellow prisoner ALBERT SPEER made this entry in his diary:

Today at breakfast Schirach and Hess refused to eat their eggs because the shells are cracked. They demand replacements, which amazingly enough are provided. In response to my question as to what the fuss is all about, Hess informs me: "Water on the inside of eggs is unhygienic. Think of all the people who may have handled the egg. Then all that penetrates through the crack in the egg, enters the stomach when consumed, and naturally has devastating effects. Now do you understand?"

I nod, at once grateful and intimidated. At noon Long whispers to me behind his hand that the rejected eggs are served in chopped egg salad—which Schirach and Hess devour with pleasure.

In the early 1900s some forty-four concerns were manufacturing breakfast foods in Battle Creek, Michigan. Some of the product names live on, others have been forgotten:

Grape Nuts
Grip Nuts
(for commercial travelers)
Postum Cereal
Hullo-Boena
Hello-Billo
Flake-Ho
Abita
Cero-Fruito
Shredded Wheat
Malt-Ho
Tryachewa
Corn Crisp
Korn Kure
Korn Pone
Oatsina

Hayina
Nutrita
Malta-Biscuit
My-Food
Orange Meat
Per-Fo
Mapl-Flakes
Food of Eden
Golden Manna
Elijah's Manna
(the original name of Post Toasties)

CHRISTINA ONASSIS lived an eccentric life, seldom appearing before three in the afternoon when she would breakfast on a chocolate croissant and a Diet Coke. Her consumption of Diet Coke, which she called "my one-calorie tipple," was considerable. In *Heiress: The Story of Christina Onassis*, by Nigel Dempster, there is this extraordinary revelation:

> The drink [Diet Coke] was not available in France; each week Christina's ten-seater jet was dispatched to New York to bring back precisely one hundred bottles. "Why not a thousand bottles?" Yves asked Hélène [head waiter and chief housekeeper respectively at Christina's apartment on Avenue Foch in Paris]. "Because Madame doesn't want old *Diet Coke*," Hélène explained, and suggested that he serve it with considerable respect since it worked out at $300 a bottle.

LEE IACOCCA became president of the Ford Motor Company in 1970 and regularly ate lunch with members of the Ford top management team in the executive dining room. In his autobiography, *Iacocca*, he says:

> Now this was no ordinary cafeteria. It was closer to being one of the country's finest restaurants. Dover sole was flown over from England on a daily basis. We enjoyed the finest fruits, no matter what the season. Fancy chocolates, exotic flowers—you name it, we had it. And everything was served up by those professional waiters in their white coats.
>
> At first we paid all of $2.00 each for these lunches. The price had started at $1.50, but inflation hiked it to $2.00. When Arjay Miller was still vice-president in charge of finance, he complained about the cost. "We really

shouldn't have to pay for these lunches," he said one day. "Feeding employees is deductible for the company. A lot of companies feed their people without charging them at all. But if we pay for it ourselves, it's after-tax money." We were all in the 90 percent bracket, so every time we spent $2.00 we had to earn $20.

At that point a few of us got into a discussion of how much these lunches really did cost the company. In typical Ford style, we ran a study to determine the real expense of serving lunch in the executive dining room. It came to 104 dollars a head—and this was twenty years ago!

You could order anything you wanted in that room, from oysters Rockefeller to roast pheasant. But Henry's [Henry Ford II's] standard meal was a hamburger. One day at lunch he turned to me and complained that his personal chef at home couldn't even make a decent hamburger. Furthermore, no restaurant he had ever been to could make a hamburger the way he liked it— the way it was prepared for him in the executive dining room.

I like to cook, so I was fascinated by Henry's complaint. I went into the kitchen to speak to Joe Bernardi, our Swiss-Italian chef. "Joe," I said, "Henry really likes the way you make hamburgers. Could you show me how?"

"Sure," said Joe. "But you have to be a great chef to do it right, so watch me carefully."

He went to the fridge, took out an inch-thick New York strip steak, and dropped it into the grinder. Out came ground meat, which Joe fashioned into a hamburger patty. Then he slapped it onto the grill.

"Any questions?" he asked.

Then he looked at me with a half smile and said, "Amazing what you can cook up when you start with a five-dollar hunk of meat!"

CLARE BOOTH LUCE became somewhat capricious in her later years and a few months before her death in 1987 she had a formal dinner party for twenty-two guests that was remarkable, especially for the dessert. After munching popcorn and drinking Perrier water, the company was served:

Borscht and Sour Cream
Pasta with Shrimp
Goulash
A "Dove Bar" on a stick

A successful Republican candidate for the House of Representatives, Clare Booth Luce dunks a doughnut at her 1942 campaign headquarters in New Canaan, Connecticut. (AP/Wide World Photos)

In medical school, DR. JOHN KELLOGG's usual breakfast was seven graham crackers and an apple, one coconut a week, and an occasional side dish of potatoes or oatmeal. He said, "My cooking conveniences were very limited. It was very difficult to prepare cereals. It often occurred to me that it should be possible to purchase cereals at groceries already cooked and ready to eat, and I considered different ways in which this might be done."

Later when he was in Battle Creek, Michigan, Dr. Kellogg

prescribed zwieback for an old lady, and she broke her false teeth on it. She demanded that I pay her ten dollars for her false teeth. I began to think that we ought to have a ready-cooked food which would not break people's teeth. I puzzled over that a good deal.

One night about three o'clock I was awakened by a phone call from a patient, and as I went back to bed I remembered that I had been having a most important dream. Before I went to sleep again I gathered up the threads of my dream, and found that I had been dreaming of a way to make flaked foods.

The next morning I boiled some wheat, and, while it was soft, I ran it through a machine Mrs. Kellogg had for rolling dough out thin. This made the wheat into thin film, and I scraped it off with a case knife and baked it in the oven.

That was the first of the modern breakfast foods.

Sixteenth-century royalty dining. (From an early French woodcut)

Breaking Bread with Crowned Heads and Other World Rulers

To eat and drink with kings and queens, presidents
and prime ministers, dictators, and other world leaders
is to be with them when they are greedy or generous,
selfish or considerate, kind or cruel, wise or stupid,
just like everyone else.

ALEXANDER THE GREAT died in 323 B.C. when he was only thirty-three years old. One story about his death is that his wife, Roxane (or Roxana), a beautiful dancing girl, wanted to get rid of him and, after serving him a feast and plying him with wine one summer evening, encouraged him to cool off with a dip in their pool. The shock of the icy water on the conqueror's over-stuffed and inebriated system brought on a sudden fever from which he died in a few days. Less romantic but more likely versions of Alexander's premature demise all have one factor in common: excessive drinking. Some historians say he fell ill after a six-day binge, others admit to a single evening of drinking and merry-making. All agree that his excesses, at the very least, made him less capable of resisting disease.

Alexander the Great doing the two things he enjoyed most: drinking wine and planning conquests. (Archive Photos)

The love of CLEOPATRA (69–30 B.C.) for Antony was lavish, as was her lifestyle. At a dinner she gave for him, all the dishes were solid gold and set with precious stones. When Antony expressed astonishment at this luxury, Cleopatra gave it all to him.

The emperor NERO (37–68 A.D.), whose personal pleasures always had precedence, did not permit the great fire that swept through Rome for six days in July 64 A.D. to prevent him from banqueting on ostrich brains, peas with grains of gold, lentils with precious stones, and other dishes with pearls and amber served under ceilings that opened to shower flowers on the guests.

Pompeiian wall painting at the time of Nero.

53

JULIUS CAESAR (100–44 B.C.) lived at a time that has a mixed reputation for eating habits. The picture of Romans dashing to the *vomitorium* because, as Seneca said, "*Vomunt ut edant, edunt ut vomant*" ("They vomit to eat, and eat to vomit") is probably overemphasized in the minds of schoolboys who prefer it to the more gracious customs of presenting guests with gifts, showering them with flowers and perfumes from the ceiling, and entertaining them with music, dancing, drama, and conversation during elaborate and leisurely meals.

To have Caesar drop in for dinner was, of course, a major event. Cicero had this experience when Caesar arrived at one of his country villas on December 19, 45 B.C., with 2,000 men. Cicero coped with the situation and reported the results and his reaction in a letter to Atticus:

He was following a course of emetics, so he ate and drank without arrière-pensée *and at his ease. It was a sumptuous dinner and well-served. . . . His entourage were very lavishly provided for in three other rooms. Even the lower-ranking ex-slaves lacked for nothing; the important ex-slaves I entertained in style.*

In other words, we were human beings together. Still, he was not the sort of guest to whom you would say, "Do please come again on your way back." Once is enough! . . . There you have the story of how I entertained him—or had him billeted on me; I found it a bother, as I have said, but not disagreeable.

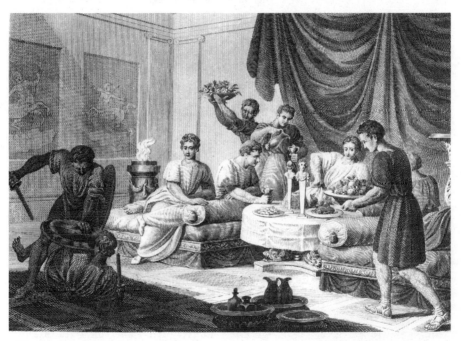

A Roman banquet with live—to the death—entertainment. (Stock Montage, Inc.)

CHARLEMAGNE (742–814), also known as Charles the Great and Charles I, used his enormous power to sentence to death those who ate meat during Lent or on fast days, which were Wednesdays and Fridays. At the Council of Aix-la-Chapelle, he decreed that monks could eat poultry only at Easter and Christmas. The monks, however, using a strange kind of logic, gave themselves special dispensation, saying that since birds and fish were created on the same day, eating them on the same day would not break fast.

During CHARLEMAGNE's time the tablecloth became an important part of dining: to share someone's tablecloth meant that the guest was the host's equal. If a guest was not accepted as an equal, the host was served on a tablecloth and the guest was given an individual place mat.

The English—and their monarchs—are known for their love of beef. Legend says that a king of England so enjoyed a piece of beef that he unsheathed his sword and gave it the honorary knighthood of "Sir Loin." Both HENRY III (reigned 1216–1272) and CHARLES II (reigned 1660–1685) are credited with this whimsy, but it is most likely that it was Charles because during his reign the tenderloin of beef was especially favored.

Charles II literally kicking up his heels at a party at the home of Lady Castlemaine (Barbara Villiers), the king's celebrated mistress. Society was comparatively "permissive" during Charles's reign, and he openly acknowledged that he had sired five of Lady Castlemaine's six children. (Archive Photos)

HENRY VIII, who became king of England in 1509, was famous for his enjoyment of food and women, but not for his manners. One of his contemporaries, Philip Lindsay, described the monarch at table:

The king ate enormously, stuffing the meat into his little mouth with a knife. As he munched, the meat and vegetables popping from cheek to cheek, his eyes shone with happiness. He jabbed his knife, greasy as it was, into the saltcellar, blew his nose on his napkin, spat into the washing bowl—he was the king. The meat was soaked with sauces of parsley, garlic, quince, pear, wine; there were great pastries, glittering with sugar, or hiding haunches of venison cooked to rags and powdered with ginger; there was veal boiled with sage and smeared with cinnamon, cloves and saffron, stiffened with eggs, all buried under pastry dotted with dates. Then came dessert of perfumed fruits and candied flowers—violets, roses, primroses, and hawthorn. Men fell on one knee to offer more things for that little mouth to bolt. Anything was thrown into it. He grabbed from dish to dish and when the food was on its way and he was forced to pause, he would seize a handful of raisins or almonds and fling them into his mouth.

Henry VIII dining in his privy chamber. (Sketch by Hans Holbein the younger)

ANNE BOLEYN became HENRY VIII's second wife in 1533 and celebrated her wedding with a feast held in Westminster Hall. The pomp of the ceremony at which twenty-seven separate dishes were served, each carried to the queen's table by a Knight of the Bath accompanied by the Duke of Suffolk and Lord William Howard on horseback, was contrasted by the duties of the Countess of Oxford and the Countess of Worcester, who stood on either side of the queen and held "a fine cloth before the queen's face whenever she listed to spit, or do otherwise at her pleasure."

It is said that **QUEEN ELIZABETH I** (1533–1603) did not enjoy the traditional pageantry of eating in public. Evidently, she got her way—at least in part. According to the following account of "serving up the queen's dinner" published during her reign, while there was considerable public ceremony, the queen ate alone.

While the Queen was at prayers in the antechapel, a gentleman entered the room, having a rod, and along with him another who had a tablecloth, which, after they had both knelt three times with the utmost veneration, they spread upon the table, and after kneeling again, they both retired. Then came two others, one with the rod again, the other with a salt-cellar, a plate, and bread:

Elizabeth I roughing it at a hunt picnic. She enjoyed English beer and ale. (Woodcut from George Turbeville's Book of Falconrie, *1575)*

when they had knelt as the others had done, and placed what was brought upon the table, they also retired, with the same ceremonies performed by the first. At last came an unmarried lady, and along with her a married one, bearing a tasting-knife; the former was dressed in white silk, who, when she had prostrated herself three times in the most graceful manner, approached the table, and rubbed the plates with bread and salt, with as much awe as if the Queen had been present. When they had waited there a little while, the yeomen of the guard entered, bare-headed, clothed in scarlet, with a golden rose upon their backs, bringing in at each turn a course of twenty-four dishes, served in plate, most of it gilt; these dishes were received by a gentleman in the same order they were brought, and placed upon the table, while the lady taster gave to each of the guard a mouthful to eat of the particular dish he had brought, for fear of any poison. During the time that this guard (which consists of the tallest and stoutest men that can be found in all England, being carefully selected for this purpose) were bringing dinner, twelve trumpets and two kettledrums made the hall ring for half an hour together. At the end of all this ceremonial, a number of unmarried ladies appeared, who, with particular solemnity, lifted the meat off the table, and conveyed it into the Queen's inner and more private chamber, where, after she had chosen for herself, the rest went to the ladies of the Court. The Queen dined and supped alone, with very few attendants, and it was very seldom that anybody, native or foreigner, was admitted at that time, and then only at the intercession of somebody in power.

HENRY IV ascended to the throne of France in 1589 and pledged, "If God wills, I will make sure there will not be a husbandsman in my kingdom who will not have a chicken in his pot."

It is uncertain that he was able to keep this political promise, but it is known that his first wife, MARGUERITE de VALOIS, introduced spoons with long handles to the court to minimize spillage on the very high collars that were in fashion at the time.

JOHN SOBIESKI, king of Poland, saved Vienna by routing the Turks and driving them back into their own country in 1638. During the Turkish siege of Vienna, bakers' apprentices were at work one night in underground bakehouses making bread for the next day. They were puzzled when they heard a rhythmic thumping. Two of the apprentices, guessing that the Turks were driving a mine, ran to the Commandant of Vienna. The chief engineering officer went back to the bakehouse and agreed with the theory. Getting directions from the sound, the Austrians dug a second tunnel and exploded a powerful countermine, killing great numbers of Turks.

As a reward for their intelligence the baker boys were granted the privilege of making and selling a rich roll in the shape of the Turkish emblem, the crescent. These rolls became enormously popular with the Viennese, who called them *Kipfeln*. When Marie Antoinette left Vienna to marry Louis XVI she missed her *Kipfeln* and sent to Vienna for an Austrian baker to teach his Paris confrères how to make them. The rolls retained their original shape and became as popular in Paris as they were in Vienna, but became known as croissants.

LOUIS XIV (1638–1715), the "Sun King" who brought Versailles to its most magnificent and made it the seat of the French government in 1682, led a life that for the most part was scrupulously regulated and governed by a strict protocol, with all acts carried out in accordance with the complex rules of etiquette of the time. Sometimes, however, his meals lacked dignity, according to the Duke of Luynes, who wrote:

During the suppers which Louis XIV was wont to have with the princesses and the ladies at Marly, it sometimes happened that the king, who was very dexterous, amused himself by throwing little rolls of bread at the ladies and allowed all of them to throw them at him. Monsieur de Lassoy, who was very young and who had never been present at one of these suppers, told me that he was extremely surprised to see bread rolls being thrown at the king, and not only rolls, but also apples and oranges. It is said that Mademoiselle de Vautois, a lady-in-waiting to the Princess de Conti, the king's daughter, who was hurt when the king threw a roll at her, threw a salad at him, fully dressed.

Swedish king CHARLES XII (1682–1718), according to a witness, was seen buttering his royal bread with his royal thumb on October 15, 1714. This conformed with the best practices of etiquette of the time because knives for this purpose had not yet been introduced.

When GEORGE III married Charlotte in 1761, the Lord Mayor of London hosted a grand banquet with an extensive bill of fare.

FIRST SERVICE

Venison, turtle soups, fish of every sort, viz., dorys, mullets, turbots, soles, tench, etc., nine dishes.

SECOND SERVICE

A fine roast, ortolans, teals, quails, ruffs, knotts, peachicks, snipes, partridges, pheasants, etc., nine dishes.

THIRD SERVICE

Vegetables and made dishes, green peas, green morelles, green truffles, cardoons, artichokes, ducks' tongues, fat livers, etc., eleven dishes.

FOURTH SERVICE

Curious ornaments in pastry and cakes, jellies, blomanges in a variety of shapes, figures, and colors, nine dishes.

According to a contemporary chronicler, "Champagne, burgundy, and other valuable wines were to be had everywhere and nothing was so scarce as water."

The royal banquet at Guildhall in 1761. (From a contemporary print)

Later in his reign, George III became so frugal that he and his queen were derided by the English aristocracy and mocked by the artist James Gillray. Eventually, however, this unroyal domesticity and parsimony of George and Charlotte was a source of their popularity with the people of England.

George III and Queen Charlotte caricatured by James Gillray as they frugally prepare their own breakfast ("Toasting Muffins") and supper ("Frying Sprats"). (The Metropolitan Museum of Art, Gift of Mr. and Mrs. Charles Wrightsman, 1980)

GEORGE IV (1762–1830), in contrast to his parents, was notorious for his extravagant and excessive behavior. To celebrate his crowning, 312 British peers—all male—attended a banquet at Westminster Hall where they were served:

160 tureens of soup & 160 dishes of fish
160 hot joints & 160 dishes of vegetables
480 sauce boats (lobster, butter, mint)
80 dishes of braised ham & 90 savory pies
80 dishes of goose & 80 savory cakes
80 of braised beef & 80 of braised capons
1,190 side dishes
320 dishes of mounted pastry & 320 small pastry
400 dishes of shellfish (lobster and crayfish)
160 dishes of cold roast fowl
80 dishes of cold lamb

The peeresses and their children looked down upon this feast from the gallery. An eyewitness described the scene:

The peeresses in the gallery, now feeling very hungry, could only glare down at these wretches of men making beasts of themselves. But round the loaded tables, not all feelings of chivalry or family responsibility were dead. One nobleman at least was seen to tie up some cold chicken in a handkerchief and throw it up to his son, who, I hope, shared the catch with his mother.

Sir Walter Scott was said to have commented, "Never a monarch received a more generous welcome from his subjects," meaning, perhaps, that since Parliament had voted £243,000 for the grand event, payment came from the pockets of the subjects.

"A voluptuary under the horrors of Digestion," James Gillray's depiction of George IV. (The Metropolitan Museum of Art, Gift of Adele S. Gollin, 1976)

GEORGE IV had a chef named BRAND who concocted a steak sauce that delighted the king. He sent for the chef and exclaimed, "This sauce is A-1!" Later, Brand retired from the royal kitchen, manufactured the sauce, and successfully sold it commercially under the name "A-1 Sauce." An interesting sidelight to this is not only that A-1 Sauce has lived on but that it is also the source of the term "brand name," which specifies an original and genuine product.

(Courtesy Nabisco Inc.)

THOMAS JEFFERSON learned to make ice cream while he was in France as Secretary of State before he became the third President of the United States in 1801. Later, when he was in the White House, it was reported that he served a hot, crispy pastry with frozen cream in the center, perhaps the first baked Alaska.

Credited with many "firsts," Jefferson grew and ate tomatoes when most people in North America thought they were poisonous. He introduced spaghetti in the United States as well as vanilla as a flavoring, and he was probably the first to serve "French fries."

Jefferson's love of fine things, including food, occasionally made him a target for criticism. He entertained guests in his spacious house with its French and Italian furniture and art and served them French food. Patrick Henry, hearing reports that Jefferson's guests were eating pot-au-feu, coq au vin, and a strange dessert called ice cream, exclaimed that Jefferson had "abjured his native vittles."

TALLEYRAND (1754–1838), the great French statesman, once asked Louis XVIII for "more pots and pans than written instructions" because he believed that gastronomy was the best possible weapon in diplomacy.

STANISLAUS II of Poland did not let the loss of his throne when his country was partitioned in 1766 interfere with his favorite pastime, cooking. He went to Paris where he lived in style in a château. One day he experimented with *Gugelhupf* batter and poured it into individual molds rather than one large one. When the little cakes were baked, he soaked them in hot rum syrup. The result was sensational and Stanislaus named it Ali Bab. Today it is called Baba au Rhum.

GEORGE WASHINGTON was blissfully unaware of the hazards of cholesterol when he enjoyed one of his favorite meals, which consisted of four omelets of four eggs each, served overlapping on a single dish: one made with apples, the second with asparagus or sorrel, the third with *fines herbes,* and the fourth au naturel.

Washington was a stickler for punctuality and said to dinner guests who arrived late, "Gentlemen, I have a cook who never asks whether the company has come but whether the hour has come."

In 1783, after the successful conclusion of the War of Independence, Washington bade farewell to his officers at Fraunces Tavern in New York City. After a series of solemn toasts, evidently the atmosphere relaxed somewhat as the evening progressed, if Washington's bill from the tavern is any indication. He was charged for

6½ dozen bottles Madeira	8 broken lights
2½ dozen bottles Port	16 broken wine glasses
66 orders Sangaree	6 broken decanters
12 orders Madeira and Bitters	

George Washington toasting his officers at Fraunces Tavern in New York City in 1783.
(Library of Congress)

We crossed seventy leagues of desert with much fatigue; the water was brackish, when there was any. We eat dogs, donkeys, and camels.

Napoleon Bonaparte's diary,
Africa, February 27, 1799

NAPOLEON BONAPARTE (1769–1821) won one of his greatest victories on June 14, 1800, when he routed the Austrian army at the Battle of Marengo. To celebrate, Napoleon invited his generals to dine with him in the field. Although Dunan, Napoleon's chef, had managed to keep up with the rapid advance, carrying a few cooking utensils, a flask of cognac, and a bottle of white wine, supplies were far in the rear and Dunan was hard-pressed to produce a meal fit for the occasion.

In a frantic search of the immediate area, Dunan found a few chickens in a ruined farmhouse, some eggs, wild garlic, and tomatoes. Quickly, the creative Dunan prepared a dish that brought raves from Napoleon himself and Chicken Marengo was on its way to becoming a culinary classic.

ANDREW JACKSON's hospitality backfired on him when he opened the White House to the public on March 4, 1829, the day he was inaugurated as seventh President of the United States. The food was consumed quickly by the 20,000 people who jammed into the mansion, tracking in mud, breaking glass, china, and furniture, and expectorating on the carpets. Jackson was forced to flee his new home, leaving through a window and taking refuge in a nearby hotel. The mob was finally induced to leave the White House when tubs of punch were put out on the lawns.

In 1837, during his second term, Jackson received a gift of a cheese weighing 1,400 pounds. He decided to share it at a public reception at the White House. The cheese was devoured in about two hours, but its pungent aroma lingered for months afterward.

ZACHARY TAYLOR's sudden and unexpected death on July 9, 1850, created a controversy that lasted almost 150 years. On Independence Day, five days before he died, the twelfth President of the United States attended a ceremony at the unfinished Washington Monument in the nation's capital. It was a very hot day and when the ceremony ended Taylor returned to the White House, drank some cold milk, and ate some cherries. Almost immediately he became ill and died a few days later. At the time there was great speculation about the cause of the President's death; some said it was cholera, others claimed it was food poisoning, and there was a rumor that he had been assassinated by arsenic poisoning. Although the assassination theory persisted, nothing was done until almost 150 years later, when, on June 17, 1991, Taylor's body was exhumed in order that tissue samples might be taken to determine the cause of death. The tests showed no indication of arsenic or other poisoning and the body was reinterred.

All cooking at the White House was done over open fireplaces until 1850, when MILLARD FILLMORE became President. He purchased an iron stove, but when it arrived it had no instructions and the cook refused to use it. Fillmore went to the U.S. Patent Office, studied a model of the stove, and personally instructed the cook in its operation.

The penchant of soldier and U.S. President ULYSSES S. GRANT (1822–1885) for liquor was widely broadcast during his lifetime, especially by his enemies. Not generally known was that he also had an inordinate fondness for cucumbers. Grant often made his entire meal upon sliced cucumbers and a cup of coffee.

QUEEN VICTORIA (1819–1901) was rigidly regal and had little sense of humor (her reaction to the Gilbert and Sullivan operetta *H.M.S. Pinafore* was "We are not amused!"), but she did have moments of deep human compassion. In 1896 she presided at a state dinner in London for a visiting rajah from India. Guests were startled when the rajah lifted his finger bowl and drank from it, evidently unaware of its real purpose. Without hesitating, the queen picked up her bowl and drank from it. All the guests followed the queen's lead and a potentially embarrassing incident was turned into a moment of warmth.

HIROHITO (1901–1989), Emperor of Japan, was twenty-one when he ate bacon and eggs for breakfast for the first time. He was staying at Buckingham Palace during a tour of Europe in 1922. He enjoyed it so much that on his return to Japan he adopted this very Occidental fare and ordered it served regularly in his palace until World War II, when, to set an example to his people, he instituted a regimen of austerity and reluctantly ate brown rice instead.

ABRAHAM LINCOLN (1809–1865) paid little attention to eating and drinking but was partial to corn bread, honey, and a good cup of coffee. However, he personally planned the menu for a luncheon at Willard's Hotel in Washington, D.C., on March 4, 1861, celebrating his inauguration as sixteenth President of the United States. It was probably the most frugal meal ever served on such an occasion:

Mock Turtle Soup
Corned Beef and Cabbage & Parsley Potatoes
Blackberry Pie & Coffee

In contrast, MARY TODD LINCOLN was criticized for her extravaganzas, which sometimes proved embarrassing to the President. On February 5, 1862, for example, she held a "soirée" that the *Washington Star* described as "the most superb affair of its kind ever seen here." However, Mrs. Lincoln's critics had a heyday, saying that with the country in turmoil because of the Civil War and suffering shortages everywhere, Mrs. Lincoln should not have served her guests such delicacies as Champagne punch, scalloped oysters, truffle-stuffed turkey, pâté de foie gras, aspic of tongue, partridge, and fillet of beef.

"Toasts to the bride were given in tea, coffee and lemonade for there was no wine served at the wedding festivities."

The absence of alcoholic beverages was thus noted in newspaper society pages describing the social event of the year: Emily Platt, the niece of President RUTHERFORD B. HAYES (1822–1893), married General Russell Hastings in the Blue Room at the White House on June 19, 1878.

As temperance leaders, both President and Mrs. Hayes established a policy that no wines or liquors were to be served in the White House. This policy was both praised and criticized and led to the nickname "Lemonade Lucy" for the First Lady.

An overdressed Rutherford B. Hayes samples seafood at a Rhode Island clambake in 1877. (White House Historical Association)

First Lady "Lemonade Lucy" Hayes was a warmhearted, outgoing person. It was she who started the traditional Easter egg–rolling contest on the White House lawn.
(White House Historical Association)

THEODORE ROOSEVELT (1858–1919) dined simply but ate in great quantities except on state occasions. His son said that his father's coffee cup was "more in the nature of a bathtub," and writer Richard Henry Dana, seeing the twenty-sixth President put seven lumps of sugar in his coffee, said, "I bethought me of the humming bird which lives on sweets, and is one of the most active of vertebrates."

After a hearty meal at the Maxwell House, a restaurant in Nashville, Tennessee, THEODORE ROOSEVELT was so delighted with his cup of coffee that he cried out heartily, "That was good to the last drop!," a phrase destined to be heard and read the world over as an advertising slogan.

While BENJAMIN HARRISON (1833–1901) was President, the United States celebrated its one-hundredth anniversary as a nation. On April 29, 1889, he presided over an elegant banquet and ball commemorating the inauguration of George Washington.

CENTENNIAL CELEBRATION
OF THE INAUGURATION OF
GEORGE WASHINGTON.

BALL

HELD AT THE METROPOLITAN OPERA HOUSE, APRIL 29TH
1889.

BUFFET

Chaud

Consommé en tasse   Huîtres à la poulette
Bouchées à la reine   Timbales vénitiennes   Croquettes de volaille
Terrapin, Maryland   Filets de boeuf aux champignons
Chapons rôtis aux marrons

Froid

Saumon du Canada au beurre Montpelier
Bass rayée à la Borgia   Truites saumonées à la Bayadère
Filets de boeuf à la russe   Aspics de foie-gras en Belle-vue
Pâtes à la Washington   Jambons historiques
Tartines de foie-gras
Buissons de truffes du Périgord   Langues de boeuf à l'écarlate
Noix de veau à la ravigote   Galantines de chapon aux truffes
Chaud-froid d'ortolans   Bécassines et pluviers à la gelée
Agneaux du printemps rôtis entiers
Sandwiches de foie-gras   Salade de volaille   Salade d'homard

Sucres

Pièces montées en pâtisserie
Gelée aux fruits   Gelée Orientale   Charlotte russe   Charlotte Doria
Gaufres à la Chantilly   Biscuits des Princes
Diplomates à la crème, Chantilly
Brioches en moules   Savarins en moules
Quartiers d'oranges glacés au caramel
Nougat parisien   Napolitaines   Châteaubriands   Meringues suisses
Fantaisies   Sultanes   Cornes d'abondance   Petits gâteaux
Petits fours   Mottoes   Bonbons

Glaces

Vanille   Pistache   Framboise   Ananas

Café

Corbeilles de fruits   Pièces montées

MOËT & CHANDON WHITE SEAL   MOËT & CHANDON BRUT
MUMM'S EXTRA   GIESLER GREEN SEAL
JULES MUMM'S GRAND SEC   APOLLINARIS

HOFFMAN HOUSE.

WOODROW WILSON (1856–1924) suffered from severe digestive upsets a great part of the time he held office as the twenty-eighth President of the United States. For years he treated himself for what he called "turmoil in Central America" or a "disturbance in the equatorial regions." Even when he was very ill in 1919 he managed to retain a sense of humor. Too weak to swallow, he beckoned to his doctor. As the physician gravely bent over his patient, Wilson whispered in his ear:

> *A wonderful bird is the pelican;*
> > *his bill will hold more than his belly can.*
> *He can take in his beak*
> > *enough food for a week.*
> *I wonder how in the hell he can.*

CALVIN COOLIDGE (1872–1933) claimed that his greatest disappointment as President was his inability to find out what happened to leftovers at the White House. When he took office in 1923, America's thirtieth and most thrifty President took steps to economize by holding breakfast meetings in place of the more traditional and expensive luncheons. At these breakfasts he served buckwheat pancakes with Vermont maple syrup. Sometimes Coolidge prepared cheese sandwiches for himself and his Secret Service guard after their daily walks. Careful to slice the Vermont cheddar evenly and to make the sandwiches exactly equal in size, he once commented, "I'll bet no other President ever made cheese sandwiches for you." When the guard agreed, Coolidge cracked, "I have to furnish the cheese, too."

A typical CALVIN COOLIDGE remark occurred at a dinner party at the White House when a chatty guest said, "You go to so many dinners, they must bore you a great deal." Without looking up from his plate, Coolidge responded, "Well, a man has to eat somewhere."

BENITO MUSSOLINI (1883–1945) had one very un-Italian characteristic: he took no more than three minutes for a meal and said that ten minutes a day were as much as anyone should spend on eating. When he assumed power in Italy in 1922, his manners were so terrible that a young foreign office functionary was given the job of teaching him the rudiments of etiquette.

One might expect that Edward, King of England in 1936, then after his abdication the **DUKE OF WINDSOR**, would be the most gracious of hosts. Alas, not so, according to the following passage from *The Windsor Story*, by J. Bryan III and Charles J. V. Murphy, which reveals Edward—and his duchess—in an unexpected light:

> *When Windsor gave a party at a restaurant, he would often try to evade his obligation as a host by pointedly ignoring the* addition *put beside his*

plate. . . . His dilly-dally tactics included staring into the middle distance, whistling a light tune, and drumming his fingers on the table. . . ."

Sometimes the duchess played a role in this ploy:

> *A penurious writer . . . had completed some ghost-writing for the Duke in Paris—a job of perhaps a week—and he and his wife were packing to fly home to Washington the next morning when their telephone rang: "Oh, it's the Dook! Will you come to a farewell dinner with the Duchess and I tonight?" (His English grammar was faultless except for this ingrained solecism.) ". . . Splendid! I've booked a booth at the Berkeley, and we'll pick you up at eight."*
>
> *. . . The American couple loved fine food and wine, but the Berkeley's tariff had kept them away. Tonight the bars were down. As soon as the party was seated, the Duke took charge and made it clear that he was playing a no-limit game.*
>
> *"We'll start with iced vodka, I think—vodka and caviar. The caviar here is excellent,* excellent! *Or perhaps some of you would prefer smoked salmon? Two hands. Good. Waiter, two caviar, two smoked salmon. I recommend a melon next. Those delicious little Charentais melons are in season, aren't they, waiter? Splendid! Melons all round, then. Now let's move straight along to the entrée. I recommend a double mutton chop, with soufflé potatoes and fresh asparagus. Oh, no meat for you, darling? Very well. Rare for me, waiter, and how about you two? One rare and one medium. Green salads, of course. Got all that, waiter? We'll see about a sweet later. Thank you."*
>
> *Visions of these sugarplums began dancing in the Americans' heads. "Pic-*

On their way from Vienna to Venice with two cars and four servants in 1956, the Duke and Duchess of Windsor stop for a jolly lunch at Boschetti, a restaurant in Tricesimo, Italy. (AP/Wide World Photos)

ture us," the wife said long afterward, when her wounds had healed, "little us, with the former King of England and his famous Duchess, in a chic restaurant, about to be served a marvelous dinner, and—"

"—and snap!" her husband interrupted. "The former King of England's famous Duchess sprang the trap. She turned to me and asked, 'Now, then: Isn't it time you order the wine?'

"There was no doubting the meaning. The sommelier was already pressing the wine card into my palsied hands—palsied by my sudden realization that it was a trailblazer for a murderous tab. . . .

"I thought of the crumpled bank notes in my pocket, pitifully few and pitifully small, and I prayed that my wife would have enough with her to make up the deficit. By God's grace, she did. We scraped through, just barely. The last ten-franc note went to the doorman. And, you know, in time I came to value the experience. It was all so smoothly done. The timing was perfect, especially the invitation to assume the honor of choosing the wine. A charming piece of footwork! I was never able to bring myself to believe that practice accounted for its perfection."

EDWARD VIII abdicated the throne of England in a radio speech on December 11, 1936. The night before, the then-King Edward had a few intimate friends to dinner at Fort Belvedere. It was not a happy occasion as described by J. Bryan III and Charles J. V. Murphy in _The Windsor Story_:

> The Fort was dark and depressing. The footmen were as surly as the butler; none bothered to conceal his distaste for the friends of the woman who had brought their king to this sorry pass. The food, half cooked and cold, they flung upon the table. It was doubtless the worst dinner ever set before a king since the pie of live blackbirds.

It was an event featured in the international press when **KING GEORGE VI** (1895–1952) of England and his queen tasted their first "hot dogs" at a picnic given by President and Mrs. Franklin D. Roosevelt at their estate in Hyde Park, New York, on June 11, 1939. The King was so pleased with "this delightful hot-dog sandwich" that he asked Mrs. Roosevelt for another one.

Much fuss had been made in advance of this picnic. Almost a month before the king and queen of England ate their first hot dogs, Eleanor Roosevelt expressed concern about the upcoming event in her syndicated column, "My Day," dated May 25, 1939:

> *Oh dear, oh dear, so many people are worried that "the dignity of our country will be imperiled" by inviting Royalty to a picnic, particularly a hot dog picnic! My mother-in-law has sent me a letter which begs that she control me in some way. In order to spare my feelings, she has written on the back a little message: "Only one of many such." She did not know, poor darling, that I have "many such" right here in Washington. Let me assure you, dear readers, that if it is hot there will be no hot dogs, and even if it is cool there will be plenty of other food, and the elder members of the family and the more important guests will be served with due formality.*

During World War II, FRANKLIN D. (1882–1945) and ELEANOR ROOSEVELT (1884–1962) were famous for their intimate Sunday night supper parties, and invitations were greatly prized by Washington society. Mrs. Joseph Alsop occasionally attended these gatherings when she was the wife of State Department official Bill Patten and, according to Maureen Dowd in an article in the *New York Times*:

> *"We'd drive our Chevrolet right up to the door of the White House, and then they'd show you up and there was the President in that upstairs study shaking up martinis, which I adored," she says. "There would be what he called 'Uncle Joe's Bounty,' a large bowl of fresh caviar sent by Stalin."*
>
> *She said everyone filled up on caviar because Mrs. Roosevelt, who cooked*

on Sunday nights, was "the worst cook in the world, you know. When she put the chafing dish full of scrambled eggs on the table, they'd be heavier than lead and Mr. Roosevelt would look so depressed."

When HARRY S TRUMAN (1884–1972) and his wife, Bess, moved into the White House, or "Great White Jail" as they called it, the First Lady inher-

ited a housekeeper from the Roosevelts with whom she had little in common. The housekeeper resisted Mrs. Truman's subtle hints and refused to resign until one evening the President, known for his directness, protested vehemently and loudly when he was served brussels sprouts for the third night in a row after making it very clear that he loathed them.

Harry chomps chicken in '41.
(AP/Wide World Photos)

DWIGHT D. EISENHOWER (1890–1969), who was elected thirty-fourth President of the United States in 1952, was an enthusiastic cook and frequently did his own grocery shopping. Some of his friends said that Ike did the cooking because the only thing his wife, Mamie, knew how to make was fudge. "I was never permitted in the kitchen when I was a young girl," she explained.

Ike flips flapjacks in '52.
(AP/Wide World Photos)

During the first term of RONALD REAGAN (1911–) as President, newspapers reported that his favorite dish was crabmeat and artichoke hearts. There was an outburst of indignation from a public suffering from an economic depression and the White House quickly—but rather lamely—countered by saying that his favorite dish *really* was macaroni and cheese. No one, however, objected to Reagan's penchant for jelly beans. It was reported that forty million were consumed at various celebrations during the Inauguration and countless more dispensed at Cabinet meetings. But when old movies were shown after hours at the White House, Reagan revealed his true colors as a popcorn addict.

Ronald Reagan gives "hands-on" attention to a lamb chop. (Archive Photos)

Senator John F. Kennedy and his wife, Jacqueline, pose nicely at breakfast on their fifth wedding anniversary, September 12, 1958. (AP/Wide World Photos)

GEORGE BUSH (1924–) shared headlines with a vegetable on March 22, 1990, when the President ordered that henceforth broccoli would not be served on Air Force One. When the press queried him about this, he retorted:

I do not like broccoli. I did not like broccoli when I was a kid and my mother made me eat it. Now I am the President of the United States and I do not have to eat broccoli if I don't want to.

California vegetable growers reacted immediately and sent a large truck loaded with broccoli to the White House. Mrs. Bush, who admitted that she liked broccoli herself, said that most of the shipment from California would be given to soup kitchens in Washington, D.C., to help feed the needy.

President JOHN F. KENNEDY (1917–1963) visited the Berlin Wall on June 26, 1963, and told the roaring crowd, "*Ich bin ein Berliner,*" intending to say, "I am a Berliner." According to C. David Heyman in *A Woman Named Jackie*, "What he actually said was, 'I am a jelly doughnut,' referring to an indigenous pastry known as a *Berliner*. The more correct phrase . . . would have been '*Ich bin Berliner.*'"

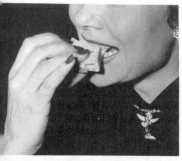

GLAMOROUS GASTRONOMES

Match these masticators with their famous names. Full-face photos can be found in this chapter.

Jimmy Stewart • Oliver Hardy • Orson Welles • Elvis Presley • Joan Baez • Anita Bryant • Groucho Marx • Jane Wyman

T H R E E

Eating Excesses and Idiosyncrasies of Famous Entertainers

Intimate glimpses of stars of stage and screen
(and some great athletes)

Actress SARAH BERNHARDT (1844–1923), or "the Divine Sarah," as many of her ardent followers called her, wasn't all that "divine" off the stage. She was a difficult, demanding, impatient, meticulous, and opinionated person who, when touring the United States, said frequently and loudly that she found American food "unspeakably awful." She had some strange ideas about cooking and insisted on stirring bouillabaisse with a red-hot poker for reasons she alone understood.

Sarah Bernhardt dining in her private railroad car during one of her eight American tours, four of which were billed as "Farewell American Tours" to boost box-office sales. (Library of Congress)

ENRICO CARUSO (1873–1921) had a big voice and a very big appetite. He was at Zinkland's Restaurant in San Francisco eating pasta and listening to a stout girl pound out operatic airs on the piano for his benefit on the night before the great earthquake and fire destroyed the city on April 18, 1906. The stout girl, incidentally, was Elsa Maxwell.

Sketch by Enrico Caruso of
Enrico Caruso eating spaghetti in 1906.

Actress LILLIE LANGTRY (1853–1929), in contrast to her contemporary Sarah Bernhardt, liked the food in America. She wrote her parents:

> The Americans do not eat buffalo steaks and bear meat. The food here is superb, but the portions so large I shall gain weight unless I exercise a great deal.

As a struggling "artiste" in Los Angeles before he broke into movies, **RUDOLPH VALENTINO** (1895–1926), like many other unemployed actors, could be found frequently in the late afternoon making his supper from the hot ham sandwiches served free at the Alexandria Hotel during the cocktail hour.

Success and a love for rich, heavy sauces quickly caught up with Valentino, and he developed a chronic stomach disorder that contributed to his early demise. According to the doctor who attended him when he died, the movie star had "holes in the lining of his stomach big as your finger."

Comedians JACK BENNY (1894–1974) and GEORGE BURNS (1896–) maintained a running battle of wits throughout their longtime friendship. In *Gracie: A Love Story,* Burns describes one such exchange:

Jack was intimidated by Mary [Jack's wife]. I knew that. Everybody knew that. Maybe we didn't understand why, but we knew it. Jack and I were having lunch at the Brown Derby one day and I ordered bacon and eggs and he ordered Cream of Wheat.

"What're you ordering that for?" I asked. "I thought you hated Cream of Wheat."

"I do," he admitted. "I really want bacon and eggs. But Mary says it's bad for you—she wants me to eat Cream of Wheat."

"Let Mary eat Cream of Wheat," I told him. "You eat bacon and eggs."

"You think I should?"

"Jack, you can't let Mary run your life like that."

"You're right," Jack said, sitting up straight. And he changed his order to bacon and eggs. After the meal, when the waiter arrived with the check, I told him to give it to Jack.

"Wait a second," Jack protested. "Why should I pay the check?"

"Because if you don't," I threatened, "I'm going to tell Mary you ate bacon and eggs."

Jack Benny admires a bunch of grapes. (Archive Photos)

Comedian GROUCHO (JULIUS) MARX (1890–1977) was in a restaurant and, after studying the menu, asked the waitress:

"Do you have frog's legs?"

"I don't think so," she answered.

"That's the wrong answer," said Groucho. "You should have said, 'No, it's my rheumatism makes me walk this way.'"

The wife of newspaper columnist Earl Wilson once remarked to Groucho:

"We ate at home last night. I made a stew."

"Anyone I know?" quipped Groucho.

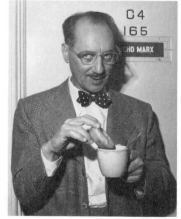

*Groucho Marx dunks a doughnut
with characteristic cynicism.
(Archive Photos)*

Comedian HARPO MARX (1888–1964) was having lunch at the Colony restaurant in New York with GEORGE S. KAUFMAN (1889–1961), one of the script writers for the Marx Brothers' classic comedy film <u>Duck Soup</u>, and was shocked at the prices on the menu.

"What the hell can you get here for fifty cents?" he asked.

"A quarter" was Kaufman's quick response.

In the play <u>New Woman</u>, HELEN HAYES (1900–1993) delivered the line "Age is not important unless you are a cheese."

Helen Hayes in the television version of **Arsenic and Old Lace** *in 1968. (AP/Wide World Photos)*

The film career of GARY COOPER (1901–1961) got a big boost when he was cast opposite Marion Davies in the MGM Civil War picture *Operator 13*, but it would appear that his healthy appetite impressed her more than his acting. During shooting of the film, Davies's personal chef catered lunch for the cast and crew of one hundred with quantities of beans, potato salad, tamales, and beer. Davies said of Cooper:

> *I'd be watching Gary and he would eat more than anybody in the whole cast. He'd have beans, and God knows he loved hot peppers, and then after luncheon he'd just throw himself down on the grass and rest until we were called. Then he'd get up and go, and he looked skinnier than anybody else.*

Gary Cooper has "chow" with U.S. Marines while on a tour of Pacific islands during World War II. (AP/Wide World Photos)

CLARK GABLE (1901–1960) had to lose weight before he was able to sign a contract for his last film, *The Misfits,* not only to be photogenic but to be insurable. He went on a crash diet of steak, tomatoes, and cottage cheese and dropped from a bloated 230 pounds to 195. Even so, he flunked the insurance test twice and was able to pass only after staying in bed for two days to lower his blood pressure.

Clark Gable digs in at the studio commissary. (Archive Photos)

When MAN o' WAR won at Aqueduct on June 10, 1920, it was his twentieth win in twenty-one starts. The 1,150-pound horse had an appetite so great that he was fed with a bit in his mouth to slow down his eating.

Man o' War ate heartily to maintain his 1,150 pounds. (Archive Photos)

LAWRENCE WELK (1903–1992) was fifty years old when he decided to go into the food business. The bandleader bought a diner at the junction of U.S. 65 and 18 in Mason City, Iowa. He redesigned the outside to look like an accordion and decorated the inside with novelties shaped like musical instruments. According to Mary Lewis Coackley in *Mister Music Maker—Lawrence Welk*, Lawrence, with the help of his wife, Fern,

> concocted a special sauce for hamburgers, renamed by Lawrence, "squeeze-burgers."
>
> A squeezeburger was to be served on a rhythm-roll with piccolo pickles and fiddlestick fries, and packaged in an accordion-pleated box, sporting pictures of band members.

Unfortunately, Welk was unable to devote enough time to the diner because of his musical commitments, and business was neglected by those he left in charge. He was forced to sell it.

Welk was never able to partake personally of his "squeezeburgers," "piccolo pickles," and "fiddlestick fries." He had to nurse a chronic stomach ailment with baby food and skim milk, a thermos of which was always at his side.

Chicken broth was fed to American swimmer GERTRUDE EDERLE on seven separate occasions as she floated on her back during her famous swim across the English Channel on August 6, 1926. The first woman to accomplish the feat, Ederle made her crossing in fourteen hours, thirty-one minutes.

WILLIAM T. ("BIG BILL") TILDEN gained such fame as a tennis player that in France in 1928 it was "chic" when ordering a drink in a bar to say, "I'll have a Tilden!," a glass of iced mineral water. Tilden was a teetotaler and drank vast quantities of ice water and coffee.

In *Big Bill Tilden: The Triumphs and the Tragedy,* author Frank Deford says:

Basically, what he ate was cholesterol. . . . All in the world he wanted were steaks, which he consumed meal after meal, and often right before a match. Some of his grandest feasts came just an hour or so before he stepped onto the court. "You should have plenty of fuel in you," he replied to anyone who would dispute him on this matter. "Better to be slow for a few games at the start because you are full than it is to be weak-kneed and shaky at the climax because you are hungry."

CARY GRANT (1904–1986), despite his enormous success as a movie star and marriage to one of the wealthiest women in the world, Woolworth heiress Barbara Hutton, was known to be frugal to the point of stinginess. Servants said that he marked liquor decanters after each use and docked their pay if they were caught drinking a soda between meals. Grant's reputation for being miserly and overzealous about getting value for his money was affirmed when an incident, known as the "Affair of the English Muffins," was exposed.

The story as reported in *Cary Grant: A Touch of Class,* by Warren G. Harris, is that for years Grant had used the Plaza Hotel as his New York headquarters and his breakfast always included English muffins split in half and toasted. One morning, Grant found three halves instead of four in the muffin warmer. Immediately, he called Room Service and demanded to know why he was being charged for English muffins (emphasizing the plural), which he presumed to be two—or four halves—and was sent only three halves. Room Service had no explanation; the assistant manager was at a loss for a reason and so was the hotel's managing director.

Undaunted, Grant went to the top and called the owner of the Plaza, Conrad Hilton, in Beverly Hills and was told that Hilton was in Istanbul. Grant finally reached Hilton in Turkey and got an answer to his muffin question: A hotel efficiency expert had discovered that most people ate only three halves of their English muffins and the fourth half was usually discarded. The Plaza kitchen staff had been instructed that an order of English muffins was to be three halves and the fourth half was to be set aside to be used for eggs Benedict at luncheon.

Cary Grant pours Champagne with panache. (Archive Photos)

TEETOTALERS among the stars:

WOODY ALLEN
ANN-MARGRET
MARISA BERENSON
DEBBIE BOONE
PAT BOONE
ANITA BRYANT
CAROL BURNETT
GEORGE CARLIN
DAVID CARRADINE
JOHNNY CASH
CAROL CHANNING
CHEVY CHASE

Anita Bryant (Archive Photos)

CHER
DORIS DAY
JOHN DENVER
BO DEREK
BRUCE DERN
ROBERT DUVALL
MIA FARROW
ELLA FITZGERALD
ARETHA FRANKLIN
MARVIN HAMLISCH
GOLDIE HAWN
KATHARINE HEPBURN
CHARLTON HESTON
KATE JACKSON
MICHAEL JACKSON
ELTON JOHN
ANGELA LANSBURY
BURT REYNOLDS
ROY ROGERS
ARNOLD SCHWARZENEGGER

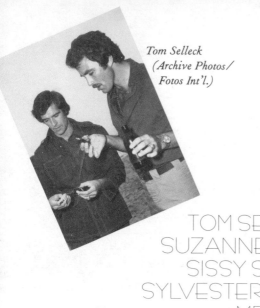

TOM SELLECK
SUZANNE SOMERS
SISSY SPACEK
SYLVESTER STALLONE
MR. T
JOHN TRAVOLTA
CINDY WILLIAMS
STEVIE WONDER
JANE WYMAN

*Joan Baez
(Archive Photos/D.P.A.)*

Entertainers who are **VEGETARIANS**:

JOAN BAEZ
CLORIS LEACHMAN
BERNADETTE PETERS
STING
TINA TURNER
ROBIN WILLIAMS

*Cloris Leachman
(Archive Photos/Fotos Int'l.)*

BETTE DAVIS (1908–1989) taking care of domestic chores is an unlikely image. Her daughter, B. D. Hyman, in *My Mother's Keeper* describes her mother at work in the kitchen in this hilarious, if somewhat cryptic, passage:

Watching mother work was more tiring by far than doing the work oneself, particularly if it happened to be cooking. When mother cooked in her own house, one didn't see the production she made out of the simplest things (largely because no one was ever allowed in her kitchen), but now she was in my *kitchen and pure nervousness forced me to watch her every move. Rather than try to describe her technique in general terms, I'll detail in full her preparation of lunch on the first day.*

Stouffer's frozen macaroni and cheese—the directions on the box read "Place in oven, uncovered and still frozen, for 35 minutes at 375 and serve." Here are my mother's directions, based on the way she did it that morning:

Bette Davis and her husband, Gary Merrill, cut her forty-third birthday cake in England on the set of Another Man's Poison, *which they were making together in 1951. The two small cakes were for the actress's children. (Archive Photos)*

Cover a counter with several layers of paper towels and place frozen casseroles thereon; remove covers and allow to thaw.

Cover another counter with several layers of paper towels, slice a large tomato and leave slices on towels.

Sit on stool, smoke nervously and sip from drink hidden behind flour canister while you watch casseroles thaw.

WARNING—do not take eyes off casseroles or they will fail to thaw properly.

When casseroles are fully thawed, get large casserole dish and tip thawed casseroles into it. Thoroughly mush around with forefinger until satisfied.

Sprinkle with bread crumbs and arrange tomato slices around edge.

Hold lengthy debate with interested parties as to exact time dish is to be served.

WARNING—macaroni and cheese is very tricky and must be done just right.

Preheat oven for 45 minutes at 375, meanwhile moving casserole dish around counter and to different counters to facilitate blending.

Place casserole dish in oven for 35 minutes.

Announce lunch loudly and serve, chewing bottom lip in concentration.

Fidget until praised for efforts, then remind others that macaroni and cheese is tricky *and requires* some little work.

When JIMMY STEWART (1908–) first started at MGM at $350 a week, a studio producer's reaction to seeing the new property was "My God, you're skinny!" Six feet, three and one-half inches tall, Stewart weighed 130 pounds and was assigned to a bodybuilder to put on weight. Told to drink milk shakes and eat banana splits, Stewart says in his autobiography:

> *I had dozens of them. I was lucky that at the time they cost less than a dime apiece. But even then it took a big chunk out of my budget. I hadn't received my first paycheck yet. Hank Fonda also helped me gain some weight.*

> *He, too, was very skinny, and someone told him that milk mixed with brandy was a very good way to add pounds. We started with a lot of milk and a little bit of brandy. Then some more. Soon the color got darker and darker. We used to drink that concoction for breakfast and by 8 A.M. we were half stoned. Anyway, I gained some weight.*

Jimmy Stewart takes a bite of cake at a celebration of his seventy-fifth birthday in his home town, Indiana, Pennsylvania, on May 20, 1983. (AP/World Wide Photos)

OLIVER HARDY (1892–1957), the larger member of the comedy team Laurel and Hardy, had a great appetite all his life and weighed 250 pounds when he was fourteen. Once he ran away from military school because, he said, they did not feed him enough. He refused to return until his mother made him twenty baking powder biscuits, which he ate at one sitting.

Oliver Hardy in 1949 with his hands—and mouth—full. (Archive Photos)

Baseball player BABE RUTH (1895–1948) was a great athlete who performed incredible feats *in spite of* the food and drink he consumed. He indulged himself to such an extent that in 1925 it almost killed him. The crisis was described by Paul Gallico in an article written for *Vanity Fair* in 1932:

. . . there never had been any complaint about Ruth's modesty. The only walls he has known have been the parallel columns of the newspaper. Even his sins are public and certainly his explanations have been notably so. In 1925 at Asheville, North Carolina, he fell victim to the gluttony that has beset him for years—the gluttony one is liable to find in a poor boy who has never had enough good things to eat and suddenly finds himself with money to eat all he wants. Now gluttony with Ruth is not your stuffy napkin-in-collar, bring-me-a-steak-smothered-in-pork-chops kind. The beginning of the tummyache that was felt around the world was engineered by a wayside collation consisting of nine or ten greasy railroad-station frankfurters mounted on papier-mâché rolls, and washed down with some eight bottles of green, red, and yellow soda pop. Anyway, they shipped him up North on a stretcher, and a whole nation trembled with every turn of the wheels that brought him home. He was tucked into a cot in St. Vincent's Hospital, in grave danger of relinquishing his hold upon his great, mortal body, and hung between life and death for many days—on Page One. Bulletins were issued from the sickroom, little boys brought nosegays, or congregated outside the high walls of the hospital and looked up at the windows of the room wherein lay the stricken hero. The presses lay in wait with pages of obituaries, and editorials announced the impending catastrophe as a national calamity. Even in England, the penny papers

watched at his bedside. That IS fame. He recovered, and the nation sent a great sigh of honest relief up into the ether. [Courtesy Vanity Fair. *Copyright © 1932 (renewed 1959) by The Condé Nast Publications Inc.]*

In 1920 a new candy bar, BABY RUTH, rocketed the Curtiss Candy Company from a struggling low-volume manufacturer producing such confections as Curtiss Ostrich Eggs, Curtiss Peter Pan, Curtiss Milk Nut Loaf, and Curtiss Coconut Grove, to industry leadership.

Contrary to widespread belief, the candy bar was not named after Babe Ruth, who at the time had just joined the New York Yankees and was not a full-fledged star. The fact is that the Baby Ruth candy bar was named after the daughter of former President Grover Cleveland, who was remembered as the nation's pet.

Baby Ruth, a candy bar named for a baby, not a ballplayer. (Photo by Meldrum)

"DIZZY" DEAN (1911–1974), a great baseball player and enthusiastic consumer of ballpark cuisine, had this to say about the eating habits of YOGI BERRA (1925–), the famous catcher:

That there Yogi Berra is the heartiest-eating ballplayer I have ever knowed since Babe Ruth. Yogi needs a half-dozen hot dogs and three or four bags of popcorn just to keep going during a game. Then he's ready for the biggest plate of spaghetti in town after the game. I'd rather take a span of mules to feed than Yogi.

WILLIE MAYS (1931–), considered by many experts to be the best all-around baseball player the game has ever seen, neither smoked nor drank, but his eating habits were not always so pure:

"We'd get into town and it would rain and we wouldn't have any money for maybe three days," Mays said, describing the time when he was seventeen and playing shortstop and first base for the Chattanooga Choo-Choos, a "Negro" minor league club. "We'd eat loaves of stale bread and sardines and crackers and RC Cola."

ORSON WELLES (1915–1985) fought a losing battle against obesity while creating constant controversy in radio, on the stage, and in movies and television. He tried many diets, including one when he ate nothing but bananas and drank milk, but invariably cheated. While rehearsing a play, he would sit on a high stool in the orchestra pit and devour huge steaks smothered in mushrooms sent in from a nearby restaurant. Then, pathetically, he would have half a grapefruit for dessert.

Orson Welles in the 1953 Paramount release The Man, the Beast, and the Virtue, *in which he played the Beast. (AP/Wide World Photos)*

In his book *Tracy and Hepburn: An Intimate Memoir*, Garson Kanin delightfully reveals actress **KATHARINE HEPBURN**'s (1907–) unique character:

I had never before seen anyone eat raw corn. At Faraway Meadows, in Connecticut, our farmer had planted a small cornfield. Kate wanted to see it. She examined the stalks carefully, admiringly, stopped, tore an ear of corn from a stalk, shucked it expertly, and began to eat it.

"What are you doing?" I asked.

"Eating corn," she said, "Why?"

"Like that?"

"Best way," she replied, "if it's fresh—ten minutes off the stalk and it's no good raw."

She prepared another ear and offered it to me.

"No, thanks."

She ate it herself.

I had refused only because I was afraid she might be right.

The next morning I went out into the field myself and tried it. She had been right.

Katharine Hepburn relaxes with a cup of tea while making The Lion in Winter *in Ireland with Peter O'Toole in 1967. (Archive Photos)*

INGRID BERGMAN (1915–1982), already an established star in Europe, came to New York in 1939 when she was twenty-four. Rather than requesting Chateaubriand at the Stork Club or supper at El Morocco, Ingrid discovered Schrafft's and happily devoured hot fudge sundaes with an appetite that alarmed her American hosts.

Ingrid Bergman eats shirred eggs and rye bread, looking as though she would rather have a hot fudge sundae. (Archive Photos)

The story of JUDY GARLAND (1922–1969) is a frightening one of a talented girl of ten, with a passion for pistachio ice cream and hot dogs, who was driven to a mental and physical breakdown by diets and drugs. As soon as she was under contract at MGM, Louis B. Mayer issued the manifesto, "Groom that child and slim her."

In *Judy Garland: A Biography,* author Anne Edwards outlines how studio doctors gave her diet pills that helped her lose weight but made sleeping difficult. Seconal was prescribed to cure that. When she was fourteen, Judy was on a diet of chicken soup and black coffee, she smoked four packs of cigarettes a day to fight her appetite, and took pills every four hours.

FRANK SINATRA (1915–) has been heard to rave about the favorite foods—spaghetti and lemon pie—that Nancy, his first wife, prepared for him during the years he struggled to become recognized. Later, when he was internationally famous, he was more difficult to please. Kitty Kelley, in *His Way: The Unauthorized Biography of Frank Sinatra,* includes this description by a friend of Sinatra's:

"George Jacobs [Sinatra's valet] was preparing spaghetti pomodoro, Frank's favorite, . . . we sat down to dinner and George started serving the spaghetti. Frank took one forkful and then started yelling that it was not prepared properly. George stood there quaking in his boots, not saying a word as Frank seized the platter and threw it in his face, screaming, 'You eat it. You eat this crap. I won't!' George didn't flinch. He just peeled the spaghetti off his face

and went back to the kitchen. I was so
stunned by what Frank had done that I
could barely speak. Finally, I said, 'That
was unkind. A very unkind thing to do.'
He yelled. 'Goddam it. That bastard
doesn't know how to cook al dente and
that's the only way I'll eat it!'"

*Frank Sinatra struggles with a
domestic problem. (Archive Photos)*

MARGOT FONTEYN (1919–1991) had a problem with food from the moment she was born. The great prima ballerina talks about it in her autobiography:

> *I had a stubborn rebellious streak that manifested itself most strongly on the question of food. Here I had certain eccentric preferences, and very strong dislikes, which nothing in the world could force me to overcome. As the dislikes included meat, fish, vegetables, eggs and milk, my mother was extremely concerned about me until the family doctor observed, "She looks healthy enough, so let her be."*
>
> *Thereafter she stopped worrying as she left me in the charge of a waitress at Paul's Tea Shop in Ealing Broadway while she went shopping; and there I would eat my way methodically through as many doughnuts as I could in her absence, usually at least six, always biting carefully round the jammy center and saving it till last. I sat alone at the table near the Art Nouveau fireplace, gazing at a large china cat with a very elongated neck and getting my fingers incredibly sticky. I never uttered a word except to say, "Yes please," when the waitress offered more doughnuts.*

As a budding ballet star Margot Fonteyn began to receive dinner invitations:

> *The first dinner did not go too well, for when confronted by the restaurant menu I realized that I had never in my life tasted any of the dishes offered. Heinz baked beans on toast were not served at the Savoy Grill. Rather lamely, I said I would have the same as my host, and this turned out to be sole meunière. Slicing recklessly into the unfamiliar object on my plate, I ended up*

with a mouthful of bones. The rather astonished young man found himself giving me a lesson in how to eat fish.

Dame Margot Fonteyn
in London in 1965.
(AP/Wide World Photos)

PAUL NEWMAN (1925– , markets his own salad dressing, salsa, popcorn, and "industrial strength" spaghetti sauce and donates all profits to charity. He drives fast, chugalugs beer, will not sign autographs, is a popcorn addict, and eats watermelon in the shower.

In his autobiography, *This Life*, SIDNEY POITIER (1927–) describes his childhood on Cat Island in the Bahamas where his father grew tomatoes, string beans, sweet potatoes, yams, okra, peppers, and corn fertilized with bat excrement:

> *Corn was the foundation of our diet—the center of almost every meal. It was roasted, toasted, baked, broiled, stewed, and ground into grits by a small hand-operated grinder, but first it had to be plucked, shucked, and dried in the sun until the kernels, hard as pebbles, could be easily rubbed from the cob. Grits and fish, roast corn and fish, grits with eggs, chicken and grits—cornmeal cereal and condensed milk. Whatever the time of day, whatever the meal, corn made its appearance.*

GRACE KELLY (1928–1982) married Prince Rainier of Monaco in 1956 in one of the most publicized weddings of the century. The wedding reception for over six hundred guests was held in the palace courtyard where Champagne flowed and enormous tables held caviar, smoked salmon, shrimp, ham, salami, soup, cheese, jellied eggs, cold lobster, and chicken. The celebration concluded when the couple cut a five-tier wedding cake, which was taller than either of them, with the prince's sword.

Grace Kelly is charmingly domestic in 1953. (Archive Photos/Livitsanos)

Priscilla Beaulieu Presley, the wife of ELVIS PRESLEY (1935– 1977), tells about her famous husband's eating preferences in her book *Elvis and Me:*

Every night before dinner was served, I came downstairs first, checked with the maids to see that his food was just the way he liked it—his mashed potatoes creamily whipped, plenty of cornbread, and his meat burned to perfection. . . .

I decided one evening to show off my cooking skills for everyone by making one of Elvis's favorite dishes, lasagna. . . . I tried to appear cool and confident as I brought out the fancily prepared platter and started cutting individual squares for my guests. I did notice that when I started slicing the lasagna, it felt a little tough, but thinking I was holding a dull knife, I continued dishing it out.

I sat down, smiled anxiously, and said, "Please start." We all took a bite and—crunch. There was a look of shock on everyone's face. I looked at my plate and was mortified when I realized I had forgotten to boil the pasta.

Elvis began laughing, but when he saw I was about to cry he turned to his plate and began eating, uncooked noodles and all. Taking their lead from him, everyone followed suit.

Elvis Presley with sandwich. (Archive Photos)

JOHN LENNON (1940–1980), leader of The Beatles, was shot and killed by Mark David Chapman outside the Dakota apartment house in New York City on December 8, 1980. Members of the medical team at Roosevelt Hospital who tried to resuscitate Lennon were aghast at his very poor physical condition that verged on acute malnutrition, caused by Lennon's constant self-abuse with drugs, liquor, and faddish diets.

LAURENCE OLIVIER (1907–1989) wrote a book, *Confessions of an Actor*, but resisted efforts by his publisher to go on a tour promoting its sale. Donald Spoto, author of *Olivier: A Biography*, tells the story:

> *Dining with his American publisher Michael Korda and agent Milton Goldman (Laurence Evans's New York colleague at ICM), Olivier was determined that his public appearances on behalf of the book would be at his own discretion, and to that end he acted the part of a slightly dotty Englishman visiting America for the first time. What exactly was a baked potato? he asked the waiter at Gallagher's. And hash browns? Lyonnaise? Cottage fries? He then ordered all eight varieties on the menu. . . . Korda soon realized that Olivier simply did not want to embark on a lengthy publicity tour, and so he assumed the role of a man who could not possibly appear in public.*

HUMPHREY BOGART (1899–1957) followed a regular routine when making a movie, according to Nathaniel Benchley, author of the biography *Humphrey Bogart*:

He came to work with a lunchbox containing two sandwiches and a bottle of beer; he'd take these to his dressing room or trailer, and when the lunch break came he would divide it evenly, a half hour for the sandwiches and beer, and a half hour for a nap.

While filming *The African Queen*, Bogart,

cheerfully ignoring Miss Hepburn's lectures about drinking, maintained a steady diet of baked beans, canned asparagus, and Scotch whisky, and later claimed that whenever a fly bit him it dropped dead.

Bogart was especially fond of Drambuie:

Apropos the Drambuie, once when the Bogarts had gone to New York, a friend in Hollywood went into Romanoff's and asked John, the bartender, if they had yet returned. John glanced at the oversized Drambuie bottle on the back of the bar, quickly estimated its contents, and said, "No, sir, Mr. Bogart's not back yet."

Mr. and Mrs. Humphrey Bogart (Lauren Bacall) enjoy a meal and each other at the Stork Club. (Archive Photos)

Samuel Johnson was a steady patron at the Mitre Tavern and liked to linger there until late, drinking port with friends such as his biographer James Boswell and author Oliver Goldsmith. (From an engraving by R. B. Parkes, after the painting by Eyre Crowe, A.R.A.)

FOUR

Consuming Passions of Creative People

Writers, artists, composers—because they spend so much time alone—take eating and drinking seriously when they emerge from their solitude, where, it is evident, their thoughts were frequently occupied with food and drink.

HORACE (65–8 B.C.), the Roman poet and satirist, evidently did not enjoy eating out because

The stomach heaves when one receives from a valet a goblet bearing the greasy print of his sauce-stained fingers, and when one sees at the bottom the filthy dregs collected there.

The Roman scholar PLINY (23–79 A.D.) made this comment about beer: "The people of the West get drunk on moldy grain."

VOLTAIRE (François-Marie Arouet, 1694–1778) had sensible, but sometimes extreme, ideas about his health, which fluctuated according to the degree of his success and happiness. In 1723, during an epidemic of smallpox that killed one-third of the population of Paris, Voltaire contracted the disease. He attributed his recovery to the self-administration of a series of emetics and two hundred pints of lemonade.

The Mitre Tavern in Fleet Street, London, was a favorite meeting, eating, and drinking place of the literati in the eighteenth century. WILLIAM HOGARTH (1697–1764), acclaimed in his lifetime as a great "pictorial dramatist" for his famous series *A Harlot's Progress, A Rake's Progress, Marriage à la Mode,* and *The Election,* entertained at the Mitre with charming invitations such as the one below to a Mr. King, asking him to join Hogarth at the Mitre to "eat a bit of pie."

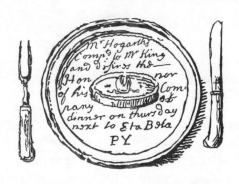

From Biographical Anecdotes *by Nichol,
first published in 1781)*

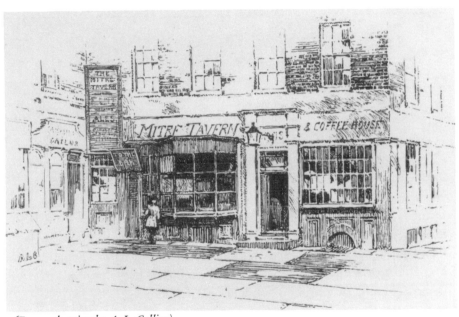

(From a drawing by A. L. Collins)

'Tis not the drinking that is to be blamed, but the excess.

Table Talk, by John Selden (1584–1654)

Drink not the third glass—
which thou canst not tame
When once it is within thee.

"The Church Porch,"
by George Herbert (1593–1633)

WILLIAM HOGARTH unmercifully included well-known people in his pictures. In *A Midnight Modern Conversation,* he portrayed Parson Ford, a kinsman of Samuel Johnson, ladling punch at a drunken brawl. Johnson was more than kind when asked by James Boswell about Parson Ford, saying, "I have been told he was a man of many parts; very profligate, but I never heard he was impious." Ford, because of his licentiousness, fell into disgrace.

A Midnight Modern Conversation, *by William Hogarth, was published in 1733 and is typical of many of his engravings in that it shows well-known personages in circumstances they would have preferred not made public.*

SAMUEL JOHNSON (1709–1784), the famous English lexicographer and author, found it difficult to stop drinking once he had started, and he attempted to abstain entirely. His wisdom and thoughtfulness on the subject of drinking were revealed in an entry by James Boswell in his famous journal on March 16, 1776, which says in part:

> *I heard him once give a very judicious practical advice upon this subject: "A man who has been drinking wine at all freely, should never go into new company. With those who have partaken wine with him, he may be pretty well in unison; but he will, probably, be offensive or appear ridiculous to other people."*

. . . it's Johnson's habit, even when eating out, to eat in silence himself, concentrating on his food with a gluttonous intensity, so totally absorbed in it that "his looks seemed rivetted to the plate." Unless in very high company, [he would not] say one word or even pay the least attention to what was said by others, till he had satisfied his appetite, which was so fierce, and indulged with such intenseness, that while in the act of eating, the veins of his forehead swelled, and generally a strong perspiration was visible.

Life of Johnson, by James Boswell

Samuel Johnson having tea with Mr. and Mrs. James Boswell.
(Etching by Thomas Rowlandson)

BENJAMIN FRANKLIN (1706–1790) gave a lot of thought to wine and drinking and was at his humorous best in the letter "On Wine," in which he proclaimed that wine is a "divine" creation by God "to gladden the heart of man." In a postscript, he added, with illustrations:

P.S. To confirm still more your piety and gratitude to Divine Providence, reflect upon the situation which it has given to the elbow. *You see (Figures 1 and 2) in animals, who are intended to drink the waters that flow upon the earth, that if they have long legs, they have also a long neck, so that they can get at their drink without kneeling down. But man, who was destined to drink wine, must be able to raise the glass to his mouth. If the elbow had been placed nearer the hand (as in Figure 3), the part in advance would have been too short to bring the glass up to the mouth; and if it had been placed nearer the shoulder (as in Figure 4), that part would have been so long that it would have carried the wine far beyond the mouth. But by the actual situation (represented in Figure 5), we are enabled to drink at our ease, the glass going exactly to the mouth. Let us, then, with glass in hand, adore this benevolent wisdom;—Let us adore and drink!*

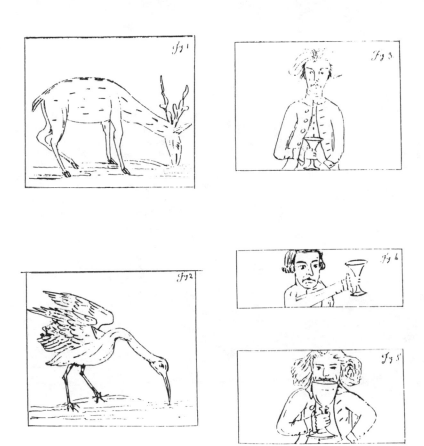

Sketches illustrating Benjamin Franklin's description of the placement of the human elbow enabling man to drink wine.

Benjamin Franklin dispenses wisdom with tea under the trees.
(Archive Photos/American Stock)

If all be true that I do think,
There are five reasons we should drink;
Good wine—a friend—or being dry—
Or lest we should be by and by—
Or any other reason why.

"Reasons for Drinking,"
by Henry Aldrich (1648–1710)

England has three sauces and 360 religions; whereas France has three religions and 360 sauces.

Talleyrand (1754–1838)

Let us have wine and women,
            mirth and laughter,
Sermons and soda-water
            the day after.

Don Juan, by Lord Byron (1788–1824)

CHARLES LAMB (1775–1834), better known by his pseudonym Elia, was widely read during his lifetime and known for his quick wit with remarks such as "A man cannot have a pure mind who refuses apple dumpling" and "An epicure eats with his brain as well as his mouth."

Afflicted with a severe stammer, Lamb avoided long discussion with puns or jokes. Once he was asked by a lady:

"Mr. Lamb, how do you like babies?"

"B-b-boiled, ma'am," Lamb replied.

JOHANN SEBASTIAN BACH (1685–1750) was so fond of coffee that he once wrote a whole cantata about it.

WOLFGANG AMADEUS MOZART (1756–1791) loved fine clothes and food and wine. Vienna became the center of his universe and he reveled in its *joie de vivre* and delicious *Torten* and *Schnitzel*. He was the toast of Prague, where he wrote *Don Giovanni* with Lorenzo da Ponte, spending many hours at the Three Golden Lions drinking great quantities of punch and pilsner beer and eating the excellent local cheese and ham. Mozart was entertained lavishly by royalty and nobility, but died in 1791 at the age of thirty-five, in debt and suffering from malnutrition.

It is evident that there was an abundance of Champagne at this festive dinner honoring Mozart.
(Stock Montage, Inc.)

In 1847 a twenty-one-year-old accountant, STEPHEN FOSTER, sat in the Eagle Ice Cream Parlor in Pittsburgh, Pennsylvania, and listened to the first public rendition of his song "Oh! Susanna," which became the most popular song in America in two years. It was said that Foster could write a song in the morning, sell it in the afternoon, and spend the money in bars the same night. He died at thirty-eight in 1864 with thirty-eight cents in his pocket and no other assets.

At an early age, JOHANNES BRAHMS (1833–1897) helped support his family by playing dance music in waterfront bars in Hamburg, where bartenders plied him with drinks to keep him awake. He loved food and said that the main melody of his Third Symphony was inspired by a meal of fresh asparagus and Champagne. His table manners, however, left something to be desired. He was known to eat sardines for breakfast and drink the oil directly from the tin.

ROBERT BURNS, Scotsman and poet, was known for his enjoyment of whisky. In 1788, when he was twenty-nine years old, he accepted a government appointment as a gauger, with responsibility for determining the taxes due on distilled liquors. This job, while it provided a living for Burns and his family, was probably the worst position he could have had, considering his tendency to drink to excess.

Robert Burns pictured at home doing a little "off-the-job" whisky "gauging." (Archive Photos)

(Photos by Meldrum) WHISKEY WHISKY

LUDWIG VAN BEETHOVEN (1770–1827) was fond of macaroni and cheese, herring, and especially coffee, for which he had a meticulous ritual that he followed religiously: he would count out sixty beans for each cup and, particularly when he had visitors, would frequently count them twice. (Note: Research shows that grounds from sixty coffee beans equal one heaping tablespoonful.)

GIOACCHINO ROSSINI (1792–1868) is almost as famous for the classic dish Tournedos à la Rossini as for his opera *William Tell*. It is said that Rossini, who enjoyed cooking and eating fully, had grown tired of the regular items on the menu at the famous Café Anglais in Paris and asked that beef be prepared for him in a special way with pâté de foie gras and truffles. The waiter was so shocked by Rossini's request that he said he would not dare to serve such a dish. Rossini told him to bring it to the table in a way that no one could see it. So the waiter brought the prepared dish to Rossini's table, walking backward or "*tourne le dos*" ("turn the back"), hence "tournedos."

Drink! for you know not whence
you came, nor why:
Drink! for you know not why
you go, nor where.

The Rubáiyát of Omar Khayyám,
translated by Edward FitzGerald (1809–1883)

153

BENJAMIN FRANKLIN published the first *Poor Richard's Almanack* in December 1733. The almanac continued annually until 1757 and was famous for Franklin's maxims, many of which concerned food and drink, including:

Never spare the parson's wine, nor the baker's pudding.

Hunger never saw bad bread.

Eat to live, and not live to eat.

Take counsel in wine, but resolve it afterwards in water.

He that drinks fast, pays slow.

Men and melons are hard to know.

Onions can make even heirs and widows weep.

If you would have guests merry with your cheer,
Be so yourself, or so at least appear.

The king's cheese is half wasted on parings; but no matter, 'tis made of the people's milk.

Fish and visitors stink in three days.

After fish, milk do not wish.

He that never eats too much will never be lazy.

Poor Richard, 1733.

A N

Almanack

For the Year of Chrift

1733,

Being the Firft after LEAP YEAR.

And makes fince the Creation	Years
By the Account of the Eaftern *Greeks*	7241
By the Latin Church, when ☉ ent. ♈	6932
By the Computation of *W.W.*	5742
By the *Roman* Chronology	5682
By the *Jewifh* Rabbies.	5494

Wherein is contained

The Lunations, Eclipfes, Judgment of the Weather, Spring Tides, Planets Motions & mutual Afpects, Sun and Moon's Rifing and Setting, Length of Days, Time of High Water, Fairs, Courts, and obfervable Days.

Fitted to the Latitude of Forty Degrees, and a Meridian of Five Hours Weft from *London*, but may without fenfible Error, ferve all the adjacent Places, even from *Newfoundland* to *South-Carolina*.

By *RICHARD SAUNDERS*, Philom.

PHILADELPHIA:
Printed and fold by *B. FRANKLIN*, at the New Printing-Office near the Market

Title page of the first issue of Poor Richard's Almanack.

ALEXANDER PUSHKIN (1799–1837) led a short life as passionate and intense as the poems he wrote. Love affairs and disastrous gambling resulted in several duels. Once, after an argument with an army officer about a game of cards, Pushkin appeared on the dueling ground with his cap full of cherries, which he calmly ate, spitting the stones in the direction of his opponent, distracting him and making him miss the first shot. Pushkin ended this duel by refusing to shoot.

Pushkin's final—and fatal—duel was over his wife's honor. As he lay dying, it is reported that he asked to be fed some raspberries by his wife, murmuring repeatedly, "Cloudberries, cloudberries!"

There was an old person of Dean,
Who dined on one pea and one bean;
For he said, "More than that,
Would make me too fat,"
That cautious old person of Dean.

Limericks, by Edward Lear (1812–1888)

Man is the only animal that can remain on friendly terms with the victims he intends to eat until he eats them.

Notebooks, by Samuel Butler (1835–1902)

WILLIAM MAKEPEACE THACKERAY (1811– 1863), the British writer, visited Boston in 1852 and at luncheon one day was served a half-dozen large American oysters (in the nineteenth century, six- and eight-inch oysters were common). Thackeray's companion reported:

He first selected the smallest one . . . and then bowed his head as though he were saying grace. Opening his mouth very wide, he struggled for a moment, after which it was all over. I shall never forget the comic look of despair he cast upon the five [remaining] over-filled shells. I asked him how he felt. "Profoundly grateful," he said, "as if I had swallowed a small baby."

We may live without poetry,
        music and art;
We may live without conscience,
        and live without heart;
We may live without friends,
        we may live without books;
But civilized man cannot
        live without cooks.

"Lucille," by Owen Wister (1860–1938)

CHARLES DICKENS (1812–1870), during a tour of the United States, was honored at a dinner at Papanti's Hall in Boston on February 1, 1842. The meal cost fifteen dollars a head and offered a choice of more than forty dishes. Serving on the Dinner Committee were Josiah Quincy, Jr., Dr. Oliver Wendell Holmes, Nathan Hale, Jr., and William Wetmore Storey.

Charles Dickens in 1842. (From a portrait by Francis Alexander)

HENRY DAVID THOREAU (1817–1862) moved into his tiny cabin on the shores of Walden Pond in 1845. There, to say the least, he lived simply. For meals he had a kettle, a skillet, a frying pan, a dipper, a wash bowl, two knives and forks, three plates, one spoon, a jug for oil, and a jug for molasses. He cooked in a hole in the ground with stones in it as for a clambake.

Thoreau claimed that he spent only seven cents a week for food during his first eight months at the pond. Skeptics claimed that he sponged on his friends and relatives and would have starved if his mother and sisters hadn't supplied him with pies and doughnuts. There is evidence that Thoreau's mother and sisters made special trips to the pond every Saturday and brought food with them. Also, while he lived at the pond, Thoreau was a frequent dinner guest of the Emersons (Ralph Waldo) and the Alcotts (including Bronson and his daughter, Louisa May). Some people speculated that it was amazing that Thoreau could hear Mrs. Emerson's dinner bell and be the first in line at the Emerson dinner table although he lived a mile and a half away. Undaunted by such cynicism, Thoreau explained in *Walden:*

> *If I dined out occasionally, as I had always done, and I trust I shall have opportunities to again, it was frequently to the detriment of my domestic arrangements.*

"I'm Frank Thompson, all the way from 'down east.' I've been through the mill, ground, and bottled, and come out a <u>regular-built down-east johnny cake,</u> when it's hot, damned good; but when it's cold, damned sour and indigestible—and you'll find me so."

Two Years Before the Mast,
Richard Henry Dana, Jr. (1815–1882)

H. L. MENCKEN (1880–1956) lived for forty-five years in the same house in Baltimore, a city, he claimed, that had incomparable food, as well as more beautiful women and more honorable citizens than anywhere on earth.

Mencken described himself as "omnibulous" and, during the "noble experiment," as he called Prohibition, he taught ten people at a time to make beer under the condition that each person teach ten more people. He hoped to educate the whole country in this manner, but his incentive ended when Prohibition was repealed in 1933.

GEORGE BERNARD SHAW was twenty-five in 1881 when he became a vegetarian. He said that the poet Shelley "first opened my eyes to the savagery of my diet." Shaw spoke of meat eating as "cannibalism with its heroic dish omitted," and described himself as "a living proof that neither fish, flesh or fowl is indispensable to success in life and literature."

Composer IRVING BERLIN (1888–1989) had a sense of humor and was amused by jokes even when they were about himself, such as one told by Michael Freedland in the biography *Irving Berlin:*

With a growing reputation as a gourmet, Berlin enjoyed more than anything a good meal at the Colony or some other really good Manhattan restaurant.

At one particular place, he and the maître d'hôtel had become particularly friendly. Berlin trusted the other's judgment implicitly and always ordered whatever was suggested or pointed out on the menu.

One evening after a fine meal, Berlin thanked the maître d'hotel and mentioned that he expected to be out of town for some time. "Very good, sir," said the maître d'. "If you have any friends who can't read either, tell them to ask for me, too."

Author ANTON CHEKHOV (1860–1904) wrote many colorful letters during his travels in Russia, including one dated May 14, 1890, from Tomsk in Siberia:

On entering a Siberian bedroom you are not assailed by the peculiar Russian stench. True, handing me a teaspoon, an old woman wiped it on her behind, but then they will not serve you without a tablecloth, people don't belch in your presence, don't search for insects in their hair; when they hand you water or milk, they don't put their fingers in the glass; the plates and dishes are clean, kvass is as transparent as beer.

A. A. MILNE (1882–1956) wrote for *Punch* magazine for many years but gained international renown as the author of children's books. When he was eleven years old, in 1893, he attended Westminster School in London where the food, as he described it years later in his autobiography, left something to be desired:

After an hour's work from seven to eight we had breakfast. Breakfast consisted of tea, bread and butter. The bread was, to me, the dullest form of bread, the butter the one uneatable sort of butter; otherwise I should have liked it, for I like bread and butter. Tea was tea, and I was never fussy about tea, but the milk had been boiled, and great lumps of skin floated about on top of it. It made me almost sick to look at that milk, to smell that milk, to think of that milk; it makes me almost sick now to remember it. . . . At one o'clock we had the usual "joint and two veg," followed by pudding. The plates of meat had been carved well in advance, and brought to the right degree of tepidity in some sort of gas-cooker. If it were the fruit season, we had rhubarb. Not liking lukewarm slabs of meat (or rhubarb), I made no sort of contact with the mid-day meal. . . . The last meal was tea at 6:15. Tea was breakfast all over again, with a few slabs of meat, now officially cold, for anybody who wanted them. Very few people did.

Note: Douglas Meldrum, compiler and editor of this book, attended Westminster School almost half a century after A. A. Milne and reports that the food at that prestigious institution had not changed one whit in the interim. Milne's account brought back memories mercifully hidden for decades of tough, tepid gray meat, gray cauliflower covered with a gray paste and

College Hall, where A. A. Milne and other young scholars at Westminster School in London have been fed a questionable diet for hundreds of years. (From a nineteenth-century engraving)

speckled with little green dots (which turned out to be aphids when examined under a magnifying glass), and gray suet puddings that lay in the stomach with all the weight and permanence of Westminster Abbey itself.

"Perhaps food *is* a substitute for love," said ALEXANDER WOOLL-COTT (1887–1943), drama critic and leader of the famed "Round Table" at the Algonquin Hotel in New York City. "My capacity for the former makes me tingle at the possibilities of what might have occurred had I the aptitude for the latter. Had things been different, I might have been lean and lusty," he added.

Lean he was not: When the Round Table was founded, he weighed 195 and was overweight by fifty pounds. Ten years later when the Round Table broke up, he tipped the scales at a gross 255 pounds. He loved everything fattening. For breakfast, he would start with four eggs Benedict; at lunch he would eat as many as four orders of dessert.

No one knows for certain whether or not the cocktail called the Alexander was named for Woollcott, but it is likely since it is the most fattening drink imaginable: one ounce heavy cream, one ounce crème de cacao, one ounce gin or brandy, shaken well with cracked ice. Woollcott was known to drink three Alexanders before dinner.

The Balance, an American periodical that no longer exists, published one of the earliest references to the "cocktail" on May 13, 1806, describing it as "a stimulating liquor composed of spirits of any kind, sugar, water, and bitters. It is vulgarly called 'bitter sling,' and is supposed to be an excellent electioneering potion."

No one is sure of the origin of the word "cocktail," but there is the reasonably plausible story about Monsieur A. A. Peychaud, who in 1793 opened an apothecary shop in New Orleans. There he dispensed a tonic called "bitters," which he mixed with cognac and served to customers in an egg cup or, in French, a coquetier. As time passed and Americans mixed other liquors with bitters, it is not unlikely that the word coquetier became slurred into "cocktail."

SHERWOOD ANDERSON's fondness for martinis killed him. In March 1941, the sixty-five-year-old author of *Winesburg, Ohio* set sail from New York on the *Santa Lucia*, bound for South America on a goodwill trip with other celebrities, including fellow writer Thornton Wilder. During the two nights before sailing, Anderson attended several parties and definitely drank too many martinis. On the third day at sea he became ill and was taken to Gorgas Hospital in Colón, Panama, where he died on March 8. Dr. B. H. Kean, author of *One Doctor's Adventures Among the Famous and Infamous from the Jungles of Panama to a Park Avenue Practice*, performed an autopsy on Anderson and found the cause of death: a toothpick, swallowed by Anderson along with its olive and martini, had penetrated the author's colon, causing fatal peritonitis.

Playwright MOSS HART (1904–1961) recalls the setting of postperformance conferences during out-of-town tryouts in his autobiography, *Act One:*

There is always a table from room service in the corner of the room, on which stand beer bottles, whiskey, sandwiches and endless pots of coffee, glacially cold and notably rancid. Since room service in hotels in most tryout towns closes down at nine o'clock, this tribal repast is always ordered by the company manager at about four o'clock in the afternoon; and although the food is not delivered until midnight, the sandwiches have been made in late afternoon and wrapped in a damp napkin, where they repose cold and wet until the conference begins. The sight of these pathetic bits of bread, no longer white but now a pale gray color, with slivers of rubbery ham and soapy cheese limply overlapping the wet edges, is enough to turn an author's stomach if the play has gone well—but the sight of them after a bad opening out of town is enough to make him physically ill. Usually, the butter has been placed separately in little disk-shaped china butter plates so dear to every hotel dining room, and during the conference, these become scattered all over the room. Cigarettes are stubbed out in unused pats of butter, and chewing gum is also dispensed thereby. If the conference has been held in the author's suite, the next morning, as he makes his way to the door to pick up the newspapers and read the first bad notices for the show, he is greeted by the sight of empty beer bottles, half-finished glasses of Scotch, and cigarette stubs swimming in melted butter. I have always considered it an appropriate setting in which to perform this grisly ceremony, and in some way I cannot clearly define, the horror of the room seems somehow to relieve, rather than add to, the pain of the occasion.

Moss Hart (right) and George S. Kaufman (left), veteran coauthors of many stage successes, join actress Kitty Carlisle, Hart's wife, at the Stork Club in 1948. (AP/Wide World Photos)

Cauliflower is nothing but cabbage with a college education.

Pudd'nhead Wilson,
Mark Twain (1835–1910)

Dramatist GEORGE S. KAUFMAN (1889–1961) was almost as fussy about the food he ate as he was about the dialogue in his highly successful plays. He hated vegetables of all kinds as a child and as an adult. He once said that his mother "tried to sell me the idea that lima beans were filled with mashed potatoes, but I was a pretty bright child. One bean was enough."

No one was exempt from Kaufman's amusing but frequently sarcastic remarks, including the Averell Harrimans, who, in the mid-1930s, gave annual Thanksgiving dinners in their huge mansion atop the mountain they owned overlooking the Hudson River in New York State. The dining room seemed miles from the bedrooms. One evening everyone was seated and the feast had begun when it was noticed that George was missing. A note from Kaufman arrived with the butler and was presented to Mrs. Harriman: "Sorry to have missed the bus for the first course. Expect to arrive in time for soup."

SAMUEL JOHNSON's massive dictionary, which took him eight years to complete, was not without humor, to wit:

OATS. A grain, which in England is generally given to horses, but in Scotland supports the people.

VERMICELLI. A paste rolled and broken in the form of worms.

THEODOR SEUSS GEISEL (1904–1991), noted author of children's books under the name DR. SEUSS, was asked in 1977 to give a commencement address at Lake Forest College where he was to receive an honorary degree. He agreed to speak briefly and received a standing ovation for his speech of under one hundred words:

My uncle ordered popovers
    from the restaurant bill of fare.
And, when they were served,
    he regarded them with a penetrating stare.
Then he spoke great Words of Wisdom
    As he sat there on that chair.
"To eat these things," said my uncle.
    "You must exercise great care.
You may swallow down what's solid . . .
    But you must spit out the air!"
And . . . as you partake of the world's bill of fare,
    that's darn good advice to follow.
Do a lot of spitting out the hot air.
    And be careful what you swallow.

OGDEN NASH (1902–1971) advised hesitant suitors with these timeless words:

> *Candy*
> *Is dandy*
> *But liquor*
> *Is quicker.*

His verses were published widely and food did not escape his biting humor:

CELERY

> *Celery, raw,*
> *Develops the jaw,*
> *But celery, stewed,*
> *Is more easily chewed.*

THE PARSNIP

> *The parsnip, children, I repeat,*
> *Is simply an anemic beet.*
> *Some people call the parsnip edible;*
> *Myself, I find this claim incredible.*

ASSORTED CHOCOLATES

If some confectioner were willing
To let the shape announce the filling,
We'd encounter fewer assorted chocs,
Bitten into and returned to the box.

Writer AMBROSE BIERCE's last communication was a letter postmarked Chihuahua, Mexico, and dated December 26, 1913. No one knows exactly when the author of <u>The Devil's Dictionary</u> died, but he is remembered widely for his humorous definitions, such as:

BRANDY, n. A cordial composed of one part thunder-and-lightning, one part remorse, two parts bloody murder, one part death-hell-and-the-grave, two parts clarified Satan, and four parts Holy Moses.

CHOP, n. A piece of leather skillfully attached to a bone and administered to the patients at restaurants.

MACARONI, n. An Italian food made in the form of a hollow tube. It consists of two parts—the tubing and the hole, the latter being the part that digests.

RHUBARB, n. Vegetable essence of stomach ache.

We are the first nation to starve to death in a storehouse that's overfilled with everything we want.

Will Rogers, Beverly Hills,
November 26, 1930

Some guy invented Vitamin A out of a carrot. I'll bet he can't invent a good meal out of one.

Will Rogers, Beverly Hills,
September 18, 1932

Well, I can't speak with any authority on the condition of the country today, for here it is late in the afternoon and I haven't sampled a single glass of the "spirit of rejuvenated America." I have always claimed America didn't want a drink as bad as they wanted the right to take a drink if they did happen to want one.

Will Rogers, Beverly Hills,
April 7, 1933

But I, when I undress me
    Each night, upon my knees
Will ask the Lord to bless me
    With apple pie and cheese.

"Apple Pie and Cheese,"
Eugene Field (1850–1895)

R.M.S. "LUSITANIA"

Menu

Tortue Verte   Crème Chatrillon

Suprême de Sole—Palais

Mousse de Jambon—Alexandra

Sirloin & Ribs of Beef

Rice   Cauliflower à la Crème

Green Peas   Boiled, Mashed & Chateau Potatoes

Chapon—Chipolata

Salade de Saison

Pouding Saxone   Petits Fours

Gâteau Mexicaine   Bavarois au Chocolat

Dessert   Ices   Café

CUNARD LINE

CLAUS
BERGEN

LUSITANIA

FIVE

Last Suppers: Food and Its Relationship to Great Events

The smell and taste of food and drink—if only in the mind—adds a new dimension to executions, sinkings, explosions, eruptions, suicides, murders, and other memorable happenings, some heroic, others horrible.

CLAUDIUS, emperor of the Roman Empire, ate his last meal on October 13, 54 A.D. His fourth wife, Agrippina, served him a dish of tainted mushrooms, a popular method at that time for getting rid of people.

UNLEAVENED BREAD, also known as MATZOH, is made with flour and water without yeast or shortening. It is said to resemble the bread made by Jewish women when they left Egypt with Moses and did not have time to allow dough to rise.

MOUNT VESUVIUS erupted and smothered Pompeii on August 24, 79 A.D. In the ashes evidence was found of a flat flour cake that was baked and widely eaten at that time in Pompeii and nearby Neopolis, the Greek colony that became Naples. Naples is the home of pizza and Neapolitans still prepare it as they did in antiquity: a thin crisp wheel of baked dough covered with the classic mixture of mozzarella cheese, tomatoes, a little olive oil, perhaps anchovies and mushrooms, and oregano or basil.

JESUS CHRIST hosted the most famous meal in history, the Last Supper, on April 14, 29 A.D. The many biblical accounts are essentially the same as in Luke 22:7–14:

The day came during the Festival of the Unleavened Bread when the lambs for the Passover meal were to be killed. Jesus sent Peter and John with these instructions: "Go and get the Passover meal ready for us to eat."

"Where do you want us to get it ready?" they asked him.

He answered, "As you go into the city, a man carrying a jar of water will meet you. Follow him into the house that he enters, and say to the owner of the house: 'The Teacher says to you, Where is the room where my disciples and I will eat the Passover meal?' He will show you a large furnished room upstairs, where you will get everything ready."

They went off and found everything just as Jesus had told them, and they prepared the Passover meal.

There is no known record of what was eaten with the lamb and unleavened bread at the Last Supper. Certainly, wine was served, and possibly a salad made with endive. The lamb was probably rubbed with mint leaves and eaten by dipping pieces of the meat into a mixture of chopped almonds, figs, dates, cinnamon, and honey, moistened to a paste with red wine.

The Last Supper, at which Jesus said, "One of you shall betray me."
(North Wind Picture Archives)

ROQUEFORT CHEESE, according to legend, was discovered in 1070 when a shepherd returned to a cave near Roquefort, France, where several weeks earlier he had left an uneaten lunch of barley bread and sheep's milk cheese. He found the bread covered with heavy black mold but the cheese only slightly so. On tasting the cheese, he found it had a delicious new flavor and rushed to a local monastery to share it with the monks. Shortly thereafter the monks started storing their cheese in the cave and produced the first Roquefort.

The date in this story is suspect because it is also said that Roquefort was Charlemagne's favorite cheese and Charlemagne died in 814, more than 250 years before the shepherd supposedly lost his lunch. One thing is certain: Roquefort cheese gets its unusual and highly prized flavor from being aged in the unique atmosphere of the caves near the town of Roquefort.

SIR WALTER RALEIGH put up a good front on the morning of his execution in Old Palace Yard on October 29, 1618. An eyewitness reported:

His death was to be got over early, before the crowds were stirring (it was Lord Mayor's Day). Breakfast was brought in; "very cheerful." Raleigh ate it heartily, and enjoyed a pipe afterwards, perhaps none the less because he knew how defiantly callous it would seem to the king when he heard. . . .

They offered him a cup of sack, which he drank. Asked if it was to his liking, he replied smiling, "I will answer you as did the fellow who drank of St. Giles's bowl as he went to Tyburn: 'It is a good drink, if a man might tarry by it.'"

The first American THANKSGIVING was proclaimed by Pilgrim governor William Bradford in the fall of 1621. The first Thanksgiving of the Massachusetts Bay Colony was observed on July 8, 1630. In 1789 President George Washington proclaimed November 26 as the first national Thanksgiving Day. In 1863 Abraham Lincoln made it the last Thursday in November. In 1939 Franklin D. Roosevelt made Thanksgiving the third Thursday in November by a proclamation that was reversed by the U.S. Congress two years later. Since 1941 Thanksgiving Day has been celebrated on the last Thursday in November.

THANKSGIVING DINNER

HENRY I of England was an enthusiastic eel eater and on December 1, 1135, died as a result of overindulgence of lampreys.

JOHN, the king of England who signed the Magna Carta under pressure from his barons on June 15, 1215, died a year after the historic event. The cause of his death was attributed to overeating eels, but John was an unpopular king and there were suspicions that treason was afoot. Eels were a convenient culprit since they had caused the premature quietus of an earlier British monarch, Henry I.

The PLAGUE, it was announced on July 13, 1603, was responsible for the deaths of over eleven hundred people a week in London alone. That summer the city was almost a ghost town and anyone forced to stay took care to walk in the middle of the street, chewing orange peel or smoking tobacco. The price of rosemary, which was also considered a preventive, soared from twelve pence an armful to six shillings (seventy-two pence) for a small bunch.

Mary, Queen of Scots, bids farewell to her friends and servants on the eve of her execution in 1587. (Archive Photos)

MARY, QUEEN OF SCOTS, was beheaded on February 8, 1587, having been charged with plotting the murder of Queen Elizabeth I. On the eve of her execution, she ate little of the dinner served with great emotion by her servants. When the meal was over, it is reported, the queen asked her servants to drink with her, ". . . and they did so, kneeling before her, their tears mingling with the wine."

The BOSTON TEA PARTY was staged on December 16, 1773, when Bostonians disguised themselves as Indians and dumped 342 chests of British tea into the harbor to emphasize their refusal to pay the tax Parliament had levied on their favorite brew. The value of the 342 chests of tea was estimated at 18,000 pounds.

Destruction of tea, Boston Harbor, December 16, 1773. (Archive Photos)

The PUMPKIN is the American symbol for Thanksgiving mainly because it is one of the few growing things that survive aboveground so late in November.

POPCORN was introduced to English colonists at the first Thanksgiving of the Massachusetts Bay Colony in 1630 by Quadequina, brother of Massasoit, whose contribution to the dinner was a deerskin bag containing several bushels of the "popped" corn.

AMERICAN INDIANS introduced early colonists to green beans, potatoes, onions, peanuts, plums, a variety of berries, and maple syrup. The colonists also learned from the Indians how to prepare succotash, hominy, Indian pudding, and other dishes that have become American classics.

The soldiers in GEORGE WASHINGTON's Continental Army were hungry, cold, and miserable when they camped at Valley Forge, Pennsylvania, for the winter of 1777–78. Even worse, the men were deserting at an alarming rate. Washington begged a cook to prepare something that would relieve the hunger of his men. The cook protested that he had little to work with but gathered what scraps he could find, including some tripe from a local butcher, threw them in a pot with peppercorns, and produced a hearty soup. It was said—probably by the cook—that the men's spirits were so heightened that they cried out, "Bring on the Red Coats!" One thing *is* true: Pepper Pot Soup came into being.

By His Excellency

GEORGE WASHINGTON, ESQUIRE,
GENERAL and COMMANDER in CHIEF of the Forces
of the UNITED STATES of AMERICA.

BY Virtue of the Power and Direction to Me especially given, I hereby enjoin and require all Persons
residing within seventy Miles of my Head Quarters to
thresh one Half of their Grain by the 1st Day of February,
and the other Half by the 1st Day of March next ensuing,
on Pain, in Case of Failure of having all that shall remain in Sheaves after the Period above mentioned, seized
by the Commissaries and Quarter-Masters of the Army,
and paid for as Straw

GIVEN under my Hand, at Head Quarters, near
the Valley Forge, in Philadelphia County, this 20th
Day of December, 1777.

G. WASHINGTON.

By His Excellency's Command,

ROBERT H. HARRISON, Sec'y.

JOHN DUNLAP

*Washington's food problem
at Valley Forge called for extreme
measures. (Pennsylvania Historical Society)*

The "POISSARDES," or fishwives and market women of Paris, held demonstrations in September 1789 protesting food shortages. The women suspected the millers of fixing prices and the bakers of giving short weight. It was during these demonstrations that Marie Antoinette is alleged to have said, "Let them eat cake!" Although there is no evidence that she actually uttered these famous words, the fable emphasizes the gathering hatred of the court, which the common people held responsible for their plight.

LOUIS XVI was beheaded by guillotine on January 21, 1793. Imprisoned by the French National Convention in 1792, Louis and his family were probably the best-fed prisoners in history, according to a report by Benjamin Franklin:

. . . dinner consisted of three soups, four entrées, three roast dishes, each of three pieces, four sweet courses, a plate of fancy cakes, three compotes, three dishes of fruit, three loaves of bread with butter, one bottle of Champagne, one small carafe of Bordeaux, one of Malvoisie, one of Madeira and four cups of coffee.

Before they were imprisoned and executed, Louis XVI and Marie Antoinette attempted to escape the French revolutionaries and fled Paris with their family. They didn't get very far; the National Guards caught up with them at Varennes, a little over one hundred miles from Paris, where they had stopped for a short rest and refreshment en route to Montmédy.

The contemporary satirical print (left) shows the royal family at the moment of arrest at Varennes. "Be damned with that," Louis says when presented with the decree for his arrest. "Let me eat in peace." Marie Antoinette, as she admires herself in a mirror, says, "My dear Louis, haven't you finished your two turkeys or drunk your six bottles of wine, for you know we must dine at Montmédy." In the background, the Dauphin sits on a chamber pot.

Louis XVI and family arrested at Varennes, where they had stopped to rest and eat in their flight from Paris in 1792. (From a contemporary French cartoon)

On the eve of his execution LOUIS XVI was of good appetite and had a supper of two chicken breasts and cookies accompanied by Malaga wine. In contrast, his wife Marie could manage only a few spoonfuls of consommé just before she lost her head nine months after her husband.

BOARDINGHOUSE KEEPERS in New York City on October 17, 1824, banded together to protest the high cost of living and voted to serve boarders only four prunes apiece at breakfast.

---

*The main building at
the Centennial Exposition,
Philadelphia, 1876.
(Archive Photos)*

When the CENTENNIAL EXPOSITION opened in Philadelphia on June 6, 1876, many visitors were delighted with the first bananas they had ever tasted. Refreshment stands did a brisk business selling bananas for ten cents apiece. Before this time, bananas were rarely seen or eaten in the United States.

The KENTUCKY DERBY was run for the first time on May 17, 1875, and mint juleps became the traditional drink at the famous horse race. Some years earlier, HENRY CLAY (1777–1852), obviously a great connoisseur of this delightful drink, described its preparation:

The mint leaves, fresh and tender, should be pressed against the goblet with the back of a silver spoon. Only bruise the leaves gently and then remove them from the goblet. Half fill with cracked ice. Mellow bourbon, aged in oaken barrels, is poured from the jigger and allowed to slide slowly through the cracked ice. In another receptacle, granulated sugar is slowly mixed into chilled limestone water to make a silvery mixture as smooth as some rare Egyptian oil, then poured on top of the ice. While beads of moisture gather on the burnished exterior of the silver goblet, garnish the rim of the goblet with choicest sprigs of mint.

It is said that COMMODORE MATTHEW PERRY (1794–1858) brought the persimmon to America from Japan when he returned from his expedition in 1854.

Commodore Perry's claim, however, is brought into question by reports that the Jamestown colonists who dropped anchor in Chesapeake Bay in 1607 were given ripe persimmons to eat by the Indians, who also made beer from the fruit.

The Persimmon. (John Parkinson,
Paradisi in Sole, *1629)*

A bird's-eye view of the World's Columbian Exposition, Chicago, 1893. (Archive Photos)

Food was featured at many of the most popular exhibits at the WORLD'S COLUMBIAN EXPOSITION, which officially opened in Chicago on May 1, 1893, to begin a six-month celebration of the achievements of Christopher Columbus, the United States of America, and the progress of civilization.

An eleven-ton cheese from Ontario and a 1,500-pound chocolate Venus de Milo from New York drew large crowds. E. R. Johnson of Fall Brook, California, operated an ostrich farm and invited visitors to enjoy the exotic experience of eating ostrich egg omelets. Actually, the omelets were made with chicken eggs. At one point, according to Sol Bloom, a twenty-two-year-old entrepreneur from San Francisco who was in charge of the Midway concessions, a crisis arose when egg deliveries were disrupted by a strike. Bloom canvassed grocers and restaurants all over Chicago's South Side for "anything with a shell on it," and for a few days the ostrich-egg omelets were more subtly flavored than usual: in addition to hen's eggs, they contained duck, goose, and turkey eggs. "For all I know," Bloom said, "they might even have had a few ostrich eggs in them."

On the Royal Mail Ship *TITANIC* on April 14, 1912, it was warm and comfortable and serene in the luxurious dining saloon as passengers made their dinner selections from extensive menus, soothed by the quiet strains of a string orchestra. Outside, it was cold and clear and the sea was smooth as glass as the giant "unsinkable" ship cut through the icy waters of the North Atlantic at over twenty knots on her maiden voyage. Within hours, 1,503 men, women, and children would perish.

In the second-class dining saloon, 272 passengers chose from an extensive menu that included lamb, roast turkey, and plum pudding. For 155 of these people it was the last time they would eat dinner: at 11:40 that Sunday night the *Titanic* struck an iceberg. Two hours and forty minutes later the great ship sank.

Before sailing on the most heralded maiden voyage in the history of passenger liners, the larders of the *Titanic* were filled with basic supplies, including forty tons of potatoes, 2¾ tons of tomatoes, 75,000 pounds of fresh meat, 25,000 pounds of poultry, and 11,000 pounds of fresh fish, as well as:

40,000 fresh eggs
36,000 oranges
16,000 lemons
7,000 heads of lettuce
1,000 pounds of hothouse grapes
2,250 pounds of fresh peas
800 pounds of fresh asparagus

Menu for the last second-class dinner served aboard the Titanic. *(Courtesy Cunard Line)*

Menu for the last first-class luncheon served aboard the Titanic. *(Courtesy Cunard Line)*

WHITE STAR LINE

TRIPLE SCREW STEAMER "TITANIC."

2ND CLASS   APRIL 14. 1912.

DINNER.

CONSOMME TAPIOCA

BAKED HADDOCK, SHARP SAUCE

CURRIED CHICKEN & RICE

SPRING LAMB. MINT SAUCE

ROAST TURKEY, CRANBERRY

GREEN PEAS   PU

            BOILED RICE

    BOILED & ROAST

        PLUM P

WINE JELLY

            AMER

R.M.S. "TITANIC"

LUNCHEON.
APRIL 14. 1912.

CONSOMME FERMIER   COCKIE LEEKIE
        FILLETS OF BRILL
        EGG A L'ARGENTEUIL
    CHICKEN A LA MARYLAND
    CORNED BEEF, VEGETABLES, DUMPLINGS
        FROM THE GRILL.
        GRILLED MUTTON CHOPS
    MASHED, FRIED & BAKED JACKET POTATOES
        CUSTARD PUDDING   PASTRY
    APPLE MERINGUE
                BUFFET.
    SALMON MAYONNAISE   POTTED SHRIMPS
    NORWEGIAN ANCHOVIES   SOUSED HERRINGS
            PLAIN & SMOKED SARDINES
            ROUND OF SPICED BEEF
    VEAL & HAM PIE
    VIRGINIA & CUMBERLAND HAM
    BOLOGNA SAUSAGE   BRAWN
            GALANTINE OF CHICKEN
            CORNED OX TONGUE
    LETTUCE   BEETROOT   TOMATOES
                CHEESE.
    CHESHIRE, STILTON, GORGONZOLA, EDAM,
    CAMEMBERT, ROQUEFORT, ST. IVEL
            CHEDDAR

Iced draught Munich Lager Beer .3d & 6d a Tankard.

197

The sinking of the *LUSITANIA* on May 7, 1915, has been rightfully recognized as one of the great events of World War I. But what of the U-2, the submarine that fired the torpedo that caused the passenger liner to sink in eighteen minutes off the Irish coast, taking 1,198 souls with her? Seven days earlier, with Lieutenant Walther Schweiger in command, the U-2 had sailed from Emden, west of Wilhelmshaven on the north German coast, carrying forty-two men and seven torpedoes. According to one of the crew:

Every corner of the small craft was stocked with supplies: meat and vegetables next to the torpedoes, boxes of butter under the bunks, salt and spices beneath Schweiger's own bunk. Within a few days the meat and vegetables would be inedible and the men would start eating out of tins. By the end of the patrol, the food would be as intolerable as the stinking smell of the overcrowded U-boat itself.

CHOP SUEY was served for the first time in the United States on September 1, 1896. The dish was created by a chef working for the Chinese statesman Li Hung Chang, who was visiting the United States. When guests asked what the tasty dish was called, the chef was summoned and he told them, "I call it, 'chop suey'—that's what we call 'hash' in China." Not long afterward, chop suey "parlors" sprang up all over America.

Lizzie Borden took an ax
And gave her mother forty whacks;
And when she saw what she had done,
She gave her father forty-one!

No one knows with certainty what happened on Thursday, August 4, 1892, at 92 Second Street in Fall River, Massachusetts, when, in the early afternoon, Mr. and Mrs. Andrew Borden were violently axed to death. Daughter Lizzie was a prime suspect and was brought to trial for the dual murder.

Although LIZZIE BORDEN was found innocent, many did—and still do—believe her guilty. One theory is that she was driven over the edge by depression. Certainly conditions in the Borden household were disagreeable to the point of being insufferable.

An intense three-day heat wave had prostrated Fall River. The Bordens and their maid, Bridget Sullivan, had felt sick. On Thursday morning breakfast was served as usual, but Lizzie, feeling queasy, did not indulge in the warmed-over mutton broth, bananas, bread, johnny-cake, and coffee. By noontime the depressing house was oppressively stuffy when the family gathered for a luncheon of leftovers that stingy Mr. Borden insisted they eat. When the maid lifted the cover on the tureen of mutton broth, the odor was so bad that she had to make a hasty exit to the backyard where she vomited. The Bordens ate it anyway. It is possible—and understandable—that the sight and smell of putrid mutton soup and fetid fish that saturated the hot air of the house was the final insult to Lizzie's senses, and drove her to commit the deeds described in the bizarre chant taken up by the children of Fall River.

BOSTON, MASSACHUSETTS, was shaken by an enormous explosion shortly after noon on January 15, 1919, and a forty-foot tidal wave of one and one-half million gallons of hot molasses swept down Commercial Street in the North End of the city, killing eleven and injuring more than fifty people.

What caused this sticky situation? The Purity Distilling Company, working overtime to produce rum before Prohibition became effective, overheated its huge tank of molasses, causing it to rupture spontaneously. In addition to the human deaths and injuries, several horses were killed when the flow of syrup engulfed the city paving department office and stables. A section of the elevated railway Atlantic Avenue line collapsed, the Bay State freight depot and several boxcars were destroyed, Fireboat No. 13 was sunk at its dock, and a five-ton Mack truck was picked up and dashed into a building. It is said that on hot summer nights the sweet smell of molasses still hangs in the air over Commercial Street.

PROHIBITION in America is mainly associated with the Eighteenth Amendment to the Constitution, which became effective on January 16, 1919. Almost seventy years earlier, however, on June 20, 1851, for the first time in American history a state passed a prohibition law banning the sale of alcoholic beverages in "drinking houses and tippling shops" in the state of Maine.

The Maine law was a subject of controversy. HENRY WADSWORTH LONGFELLOW (1807–1882), a temperate and influential man, was in favor of the demolition of the vulgar grog shops, but could not support the law as a whole because drinking, theatergoing, and opera had been idiotically jumbled together.

The enforcement of Prohibition drove America's drinking population underground where, as Stephen Birmingham points out in *The Right People,*

> *The safest place to drink became the living room where, of course, the ladies were. The ladies couldn't have liked it more.*
>
> *Cocktail parties were a gesture of defiance against those who had inflicted Prohibition on the country. They were the bold, the daring, the naughty thing to do. There was an air of excitement about these primordial parties, the kind of excitement that is generated by jauntily breaking the law. Each cocktail was an adventure, too. Depending upon the bootlegger, a few swallows might make one pleasantly tiddly or violently ill.*

PROHIBITION came to an end at 3:50 P.M. (Mountain Time), December 5, 1933, when Utah, the thirty-sixth state, ratified the Twenty-first Amendment to the Constitution, thus repealing the Eighteenth Amendment. Eight states voted to stay dry, but liquor stores and cafés across America were jammed with people buying their first legal alcoholic beverages in thirteen years.

H. L. MENCKEN once estimated that 17,864,392,788 different drinks could be concocted from the ingredients available during Prohibition, and many of them were.

The New York Daily Mirror, in its June 24, 1924, issue, predicted that the American saloon was gone forever. The editorial page proclaimed:

GONE. THANK GOD!

The wide open saloon, the "What'll you have?" the "Here's How!" and the echoing conclusion, "Here's how to ruin a young life," are gone forever.

CHARLES LINDBERGH was handed a paper bag containing five sandwiches just before he eased his overloaded monoplane off the ground on May 20, 1927, and headed eastward on his long and epic transatlantic flight. The sandwiches—two ham, one egg with mayonnaise, and two beef—and a canteen of water were all that Lindbergh had to sustain him for the next thirty-three and one-half hours. In his book *The Spirit of St. Louis* Lindbergh wrote:

Four-twenty on the clock. That's nine-twenty here. Why, it's past suppertime! I hold the stick with my knees, untwist the neck of the paper bag, and pull out a sandwich—my first food since takeoff. The Spirit of St. Louis *noses up. I push the stick forward, clamp it between my knees again, and uncork the canteen. I can drink all the water I want now—plenty more below if I should be forced down between here and Paris. But how flat the sandwich tastes! Bread and meat never touched my tongue like this before. It's an effort even to swallow. I'm hungry, because I go on eating, but I have to wash each mouthful down with water.*

One sandwich is enough. I brush the crumbs off my lap. I start to throw the wrapping through the window—no, these fields are so clean and fresh, it's a shame to scatter them with paper. I crush it up and stuff it back in the brown bag. I don't want the litter from a sandwich to symbolize my first contact with France.

Service was impeccable aboard the HINDENBURG and the food excellent. The great zeppelin was an impressive propaganda machine for Nazi Germany as it soared over New York City with swastikas painted on its giant tail surfaces on May 6, 1937. Routes were planned that would take the *Hindenburg* over cities to awe millions. Passengers were encouraged to speak enthusiastically about their flights in the dirigible.

The tiny, closet-like cooking space aboard the *Hindenburg* was claustrophobic for chef Xavier Maier, whose fine reputation had been built in the large traditional kitchens of the Ritz Hotel in Paris.

Weight and the danger of fire had the highest priority on the *Hindenburg*. All the kitchen equipment was lightweight aluminum and the heat was electric. As the six-million-cubic-foot envelope, full of highly volatile hydrogen gas, cruised at eighty miles an hour heading for its mooring at Lakehurst Naval Station in New Jersey, Chef Maier prepared the last full meal for the passengers:

Pâtés à la Reine
Roast Beef
Salad
Stilton Cheese & Fruit

This simple but elegant meal was complemented by a 1926 Baume Cuvée de l'Abbaye from the small but excellent wine cellar.

At 7:22 P.M. dusk was approaching when the nose lines were dropped from the *Hindenburg* and picked up by the Lakehurst ground crew. Passengers' luggage was piled in the corridor ready for unloading. Chef Maier and other crew

The giant German dirigible Hindenburg *burst into flames and exploded as it came into Lakehurst, New Jersey, Naval Station on May 6, 1937. The disaster marked the end of the dirigible as a viable means of transportation. (Archive Photos)*

members prepared for a quick turnaround for the return flight to Frankfurt, Germany. Everything seemed normal.

Three minutes later, the *Hindenburg* was engulfed in flames. Thirty-six passengers and crew perished, including the chef. The cause of the disaster is still a subject of controversy. In terms of the number of fatalities the explosion of the *Hindenburg* was not a great catastrophe historically, but it did mark the end of an era of travel that had captured the public's imagination in a way that has never been repeated.

"DOUGHNUT DAY" was founded on June 3, 1937, by the Salvation Army in Chicago to raise funds during the Great Depression. From that date on, Doughnut Day has been held on the first Friday in June in remembrance of doughnuts served to "doughboys" during World War I by the Salvation Army.

The disappearance of forty-year-old **AMELIA EARHART** over the Pacific Ocean on July 2, 1937, is still clouded in mystery. One theory is that the aviatrix, ill with dysentery, was in poor condition to undertake the strain of the long transpacific leg. Her condition might have resulted from eating the famous Indonesian *rijsttafel* in Batavia (now Jakarta), where she was grounded by bad weather and needed repairs to her airplane. This delicacy is a meal of rice with twenty-one different courses of fish, chicken, meats, eggs, relishes, curries, nuts, fruits, and vegetables.

SLOT MACHINES dispensing hard-boiled eggs for a nickel apiece were installed in cafés and taverns throughout Pennsylvania in 1938 to help farmers dispose of an egg surplus.

The **"BIG MAC,"** a two-patty hamburger on a sesame-seed bun, was first sold in McDonald's fast food outlets on May 4, 1968. JIM DELAGATTI, who worked in a Pittsburgh franchise, invented the Big Mac. Literally billions have been consumed, making it the most popular sandwich in history. Asked on the "Today" morning television show on the twenty-fifth anniversary of its introduction whether he receives a royalty or other compensation for its invention, Delagatti replied, "I got a plaque."

"Food was plentiful," says THOR HEYERDAHL in *Kon-Tiki*, his account of his 101-day, 4,300-mile voyage on a raft across the Pacific Ocean from Peru to Polynesia in 1947. The raft, made of balsa logs, was a replica of those believed used by the first migrants from South America over a thousand years before. Heyerdahl wrote:

If we set the little paraffin lamp out at night, flying fish, attracted by the light, shot over the raft. They often struck the bamboo cabin or the rail and tumbled to the deck. . . .

The cook's first duty in the morning was to collect all the flying fish that had boarded during the night. There were usually half a dozen or more, and once we found twenty-six. . . . We fried them over the primus stove. . . .

Even if our predecessors had started from land with inadequate food, they would have managed well enough as long as they drifted with the current, in which fish abounded and were easily caught. To starve to death was impossible.

As to thirst in a hot climate, . . . on particularly hot days, when the wind had died away and the sun blazed on the raft, we added from twenty to forty percent of seawater to our fresh water and found, to our surprise, that this brackish water quenched our thirst.

Kon-Tiki, *the raft on which Thor Heyerdahl and his crew made a 4,300-mile voyage across the Pacific Ocean from Peru to Polynesia in 1947. (Archive Photos)*

CHLOE and ALDERSON MUNCY, with thirteen of their fifteen children, came to Welch, West Virginia, on May 29, 1961, and were given the first food stamps by Secretary of Agriculture Orville Freeman in the amount of ninety-five dollars.

The food coupons shown here became effective in 1975 and have a complex design to fool counterfeiters. (Archive Photos)

Food and eating in space were matters of serious research well before NEIL ARMSTRONG, astronaut, stepped off the lunar module *Eagle* on July 20, 1969, and became the first man to set foot on the moon. He was followed to the lunar surface by EDWIN ALDRIN, JR., while a third astronaut, MICHAEL COLLINS, orbited the moon in the spacecraft *Apollo 11*. In *First on the Moon,* a book written by the three astronauts with Gene Farmer and Dora Jane Hamlin, they describe how an element of humor was introduced during the development of a decent diet in a gravity-free environment:

> . . . *during the two months preceding the flight of* Apollo 11 *Mike [Collins] was supposed to test one of the space meals every day for lunch and tell NASA what he thought. Making judgments on a survival rather than an aesthetic basis, he liked everything, but he confused NASA. Instead of marking an X in the "good," "fair," or "poor" boxes on the checklist of meals, he drew little knives and forks and awarded stars in the manner of* Guide Michelin, *the famous handbook of French gastronomy. One morning he was called into the office to interpret and be given a mild reproof; after that his checklist was marked in the appropriate boxes, with little clarifying statements added: "Rich and mellow . . . A gustatory delight . . . The perfect blend of subtle spices . . ."*
>
> *It could be that Collins had a tongue in one cheek when he pronounced such extravagant praise, but the food had become better since John Young defied the system on one of his* Gemini *flights by eating a forbidden corned beef sandwich on board (crumbs could be a menace). By the time* Apollo 9 *flew there were "wet pack" meals which could be eaten with a spoon, and John Young thought the turkey and gravy especially good. However, Young said, "Deke*

Slayton ate the same food we did throughout the flight and I guess he almost starved to death. But in our zero-G situation we were always full." There had been some complaints during the Gemini *flights about the food tasting like mush, and a good deal of research had been done to improve the quality. An army laboratory in Natick, Massachusetts, figured out a way to keep bread from going stale. At the Swift and Company Research Center in Oak Brook, Illinois, Dr. Robert L. Pavey, who held a Ph.D. in animal nutrition from Cornell, expanded the freeze-dried (and "rehydratable") menu to twenty-six meat and fish items. (U.S. choice beef was better for rehydratable meat cubes than prime, which had too much fat.) The* Apollo 11 *spacecraft had, for eight days of meals, about seventy items of food on board, including dried peaches, pears, apricots, and coffee, with or without sugar and cream, in the snack pantry—the "smorgasbord mode." It was now possible to make allowances for individual taste; Armstrong, Collins, and Aldrin selected to start the same meal, on the second day of the flight, with (respectively) spaghetti, potato soup, and chicken salad. Probably none of it would have brought three knives and forks and a Michelin star to a French chef at Chambley, but it all represented enormous improvement.*

Astronaut Neil Armstrong took this picture of Edwin Aldrin, Jr., walking on the surface of the moon after a gourmet dinner in space. (Archive Photos)

213

Recalls HENRY HALLER, chef to President RICHARD NIXON:

On the morning of August 9, 1974, I arrived at the White House at 6:00 A.M. for the breakfast shift. . . . I noticed President Nixon standing in the West Hall outside the Family Kitchen. He was still in his pajamas, but he seemed full of energy. . . . President Nixon followed me into the kitchen. He ordered a special breakfast for himself, more substantial than his usual morning meal of wheat germ and coffee. The President asked a butler to serve what was to be his final White House meal in his favorite room, the Lincoln Sitting Room. When the President finished eating his poached egg and hash, Alexander Haig entered the room bearing a sheet of paper with a single typed sentence: "I hereby resign the office of the President of the United States."

Ten years after his resignation, Richard Nixon addressed a meeting of the American Society of Newspaper Editors in Washington, D.C. (AP/Wide World Photos)